SKILLS & VALUES: TRUSTS AND ESTATES

D1500938

SKILLS & VALUES: TRUSTS AND ESTATES

Roger W. Andersen
Professor Emeritus of Law
University of Toledo
College of Law

Karen E. Boxx
Associate Professor of Law
University of Washington School of Law

 LexisNexis®

Library of Congress Cataloging-in-Publication Data

Andersen, Roger W.
  Skills & values—trusts and estates / Roger W. Andersen, Karen E. Boxx.
    p. cm.
  ISBN 978-1-4224-2698-2 (softbound)
  1. Trusts and trustees—United States—Problems, exercises, etc. 2. Wills—United States—Problems exercises, etc. 3. Estate planning—United States—Problems, exercises, etc. I. Boxx, Karen E. I. Title. III. Title: Skills and values—trusts and estates.
  KF753.A958 2009
  346.7305'9076—dc22

                                                                        2008053897

This publication is designed to provide accurate and authoritative information in regard to the su matter covered. It is sold with the understanding that the publisher is not engaged in rendering accounting, or other professional services. If legal advice or other expert assistance is required services of a competent professional should be sought.

LexisNexis, the knowledge burst logo, and Michie are trademarks of Reed Elsevier Properties used under license. Matthew Bender is a registered trademark of Matthew Bender Properties I

Editorial Offices
744 Broad Street, Newark, NJ 07102 (973) 820-2000
201 Mission St., San Francisco, CA 94105-1831 (415) 908-3200
www.lexisnexis.com

MATTHEW◆BENDER

INTRODUCTION

These materials can help you incorporate lawyering skills into your substantive Trusts and Estates class. Many cases in your casebook reflect poor lawyering; they provide lessons about how not to do things. While giving you a real world context for the abstract doctrines being taught in class, the exercises in this book offer the opportunity to practice good lawyering.

Each chapter offers a fact pattern based on a topic covered in a typical course. Most of the chapters offer different levels of tasks, so that your professor can assign one or more tasks, depending on how much time the professor wants to devote to that chapter. The exercises require you to use the wide range of skills needed in an estate planning and probate practice, such as drafting, negotiating, statutory interpretation, litigation strategizing, and ethics problem solving.

To deepen your experience, each chapter includes a section to guide your own "self-study" of each exercise. Here, we provide a list of topics we think are important to consider in each context. However, there are no "right" answers. Good lawyering requires creativity, and these answers should prompt you to craft your own solutions. We strongly encourage you to avoid peeking at the self-study sections until you have completed the project. Don't let us narrow your thinking and rob you of the opportunity to come up with a more clever solution than ours. When the exercises call for you to draft a document, we have put sample completed documents on the website, but always remember that those are only examples of one way to approach the problem.

E-MATERIALS

This *Skills & Values* book is enhanced by a LexisNexis Web Course which will give you access to online content tailored to the use of this book. Your professor will provide instructions on how to enroll in this Web Course. The online content includes a variety of resources to help you complete the exercises, such as forms for drafting a standard document like a pleading or a Will. Lawyers often use forms in practice, and learning to work with forms and adapt them to a particular situation beyond just "filling in the blanks" is an important skill. The e-materials also include links to applicable statutes, including uniform laws and specific state statutes. The state statutes used in this area of law vary significantly from state to state. We have made suggestions as to the statutes to be used for each exercise, and have frequently relied on the Uniform Probate Code and other

Introduction

uniform laws. We have, however, allowed for the possibility that your professor may require you to the laws of your state or any other specific state. For chapters that require drafting, the e-materials also include sample documents to aid your self-study.

ORGANIZATION OF EACH CHAPTER

Each Chapter contains—

- An introduction that puts the chapter within the context of actual, day-to-day practice.
- A listing of skills involved in carrying out the exercise.
- The estimated time for completing each task in the exercise, indicated by icon below, each representing 15 minutes.

- The level of difficulty, represented by 1–5 "Black diamonds."

- Your role in the exercise.
- The number of students required for each task in the exercise.
- "The exercise" section.
- "Additional resources" section.
- A "do not proceed page" [a reminder not to be tempted to look ahead].
- The "self-study" section.

We hope that the exercises in this book give you an idea of the life of an estate planning and probate attorney. Such a law practice gives you the opportunity to hear fascinating stories, interact personally with clients on a daily basis, and use your creativity in devising plans to help carry out your clients' desires for their families and their legacy in the world.

TABLE OF CONTENTS

Table of Contents

Chapter 1

THE PROBATE PROCESS

INTRODUCTION

The probate process is essentially the civil procedure structure within which Wills are enforced and interpreted, and estates of persons without Wills are distributed. Generally, the probate process is only touched on briefly in Wills and Trusts classes, because the procedure itself is relatively straightforward and because there is a great deal of variation among states in the procedural requirements. However, a general understanding of the probate process will assist you in putting the cases in the casebook in context, because most of those cases are brought as part of a probate process.

Probate procedure is state-specific. In general, the probate process will include the following tasks:

(1) either determine that a Will is the valid last Will of the decedent and therefore the blueprint for distributing the estate, or find that the decedent died without a Will and that the estate is to be distributed under the state's intestacy statutes;

(2) appoint a person or corporate fiduciary to administer the estate (the executor/administrator/personal representative);

(3) supervise administration of the estate, including settling of creditor claims and distribution of remaining assets to the heirs.

Law school classes usually omit coverage of what a probate process looks like on the ground level. Working through this chapter will help you get a sense of what is involved. In performing the tasks in this exercise, keep the following in mind:

- **Use forms carefully.** Lawyers often use forms prepared by themselves or other lawyers in practice; it is a way to save time and save the client money. However, sloppy use of forms can lead to embarrassment or worse: a disastrous result for the client and a malpractice suit against the lawyer. When using forms, **never assume that the drafter of the form knows**

1

more than you do and must be right. The form may be out of date or may not suit your client's situation, or it could be a bad form. Read the entire form carefully and if you don't know why a provision is included, or what a provision means, ask for help. The forms you will be using and facts you will be applying in this exercise are straightforward, so you will not be doing any substantial editing. However, you still need to read every word of the forms.

• **States vary greatly on the complexity of the probate procedure.** Many states and the UPC have a probate procedure that does not require court involvement after the probate has been opened. Usually, the estate must be solvent in order to qualify for the unsupervised procedure. Because of the variations in state proceedings, the exercise focuses on opening and closing the probate. Your professor may choose to use the UPC as applicable law. Please note, however, that in an actual state court proceeding, there are likely to be variations in the state's statutes, additional pleadings and procedures required by local court rule, and specific jurisdictional rules.

• **Use the exercise to understand the nature of the probate process.** The tasks involved in this exercise are not very difficult. It will be tempting just to fill in the blanks in the forms. However, a primary purpose of the exercise is to demystify the probate process. Many of the cases in your casebook began with a petition to admit the Will in question to probate, under a court file name of "In re Estate of [Decedent] and pleadings similar to the ones you are preparing were prepared and filed. The reported opinions that you read are the result of someone filing a challenge to the Will or to the estate administration in the course of the probate proceeding. Read the applicable statutes covering probate administration, think about the purpose of each pleading and how it will be used, and try to get an overall picture of the process.

• **Read the applicable statutes carefully.** Another purpose of the exercise is to give you experience reading statutes. The sections of the UPC cited above or the applicable state statutes, if you are using a particular state's laws, govern what must be filed, what notice must be given, and the like. You therefore need to read the statutes before completing the forms.

SKILLS INVOLVED: Fact analysis and development, application of statutes, drafting skills, using forms.

GENERAL DESCRIPTION OF EXERCISE: Preparation of pleadings for opening and administration of probate.

PARTICIPANTS NEEDED: This is an individual exercise to be completed by one student.

ESTIMATED TIME REQUIRED:

Task 1: 15 minutes

Task 2: 15 minutes

Task 3: 15 minutes

Task 4: 15 minutes

LEVEL OF DIFFICULTY (1–5):

◆

ROLE IN EXERCISE: You are acting as lawyer for the estate of Sallie Wright and preparing the pleadings to open her probate, administer her probate and then close the probate.

THE EXERCISE

Sallie Wright was an eighty-year-old single woman who recently passed away. Her niece Julia Wright has asked you to assist in probating her estate. Sallie left a Will naming Julia as the executor and leaving her entire estate to Julia. A copy of the Will is included below. Julia's mother Esther was Sallie's sister; Esther passed away three years ago. Sallie's only other living relative is her brother George. Sallie's only creditors at the time of her death were:

Happy Helpers Cleaning Service	$200
The Cat Clinic Veterinary Services	$100
Omnibus Local Utility Company	$300

Her assets consisted of her home and its contents, a savings account in her name with $5,000, and a joint checking account in the name of Sallie and Julia as joint tenants with right of survivorship, with a balance of $3,000.

APPLICABLE LAW: Each state will have specific procedures in their statutes for opening, administration, and closing of a probate. In addition, the Uniform Probate Code also sets forth a probate procedure. Your professor will assign a specific state's laws to apply, assign the UPC procedures, or will allow you to choose among certain states.

TASK 1: Prepare the pleading asking for the Will to be admitted and any other pleadings necessary for opening the probate, having the Will admitted and having Julia appointed as executor. Determine who is entitled to notice, and prepare the appropriate notice forms.

TASK 2: Prepare an inventory of assets. Determine which of Sallie's assets are subject to probate and which are nonprobate assets. Only the assets subject to probate are included. Determine whether the inventory must be filed with the court, and if so, what detail is necessary on the court-filed inventory.

TASK 3: Prepare the documents necessary to transfer the home to Julia. If you are using a state's laws that would require court approval of the distribution, you may assume that such approval has already been obtained. In most states you will need to use a Personal Representative's Deed. A sample form is found on the website. Your professor may give you another form to use. You will need to research the specific requirements for a deed in your assigned state (if your professor has required you to use a certain state's laws) and the requirements for recording a personal representative's deed, including any forms claiming transfer tax exemption. Transfer tax is charged in some jurisdictions when real property is sold or otherwise transferred (like a sales tax), but there will be an exemption available for a transfer out of probate. There is a link to a chart on the website summarizing transfer taxes state by state. If you are using the UPC procedures without reference to a specific state, assume your state does not have a real estate transfer tax.

TASK 4: Assuming Julia has paid the creditors and distributed the remaining property to herself, prepare the pleadings necessary to close the estate. Prepare all forms of notice required.

SALLIE'S WILL

WILL
OF
SALLIE ELIZABETH WRIGHT

I, SALLIE ELIZABETH WRIGHT, declare this to be my Will and revoke all prior Wills and Codicils.

ARTICLE 1. FAMILY

I am single and have no children, living or deceased. My family now consists of my brother, GEORGE ELIOT WRIGHT, and my niece, JULIA ELIZABETH WRIGHT, who is the daughter of my deceased sister ESTHER ELIZABETH WRIGHT.

ARTICLE 2. FIDUCIARIES; CODE

2.1 Executor. I appoint my niece, JULIA ELIZABETH WRIGHT, as Executor of my Will.

No bond, surety or other security shall be required of my Executor in any jurisdiction for any purpose. I grant my Executor full power and authority to compromise or otherwise settle or adjust any and all claims, charges, debts or demands against or in favor of my estate, as fully as I could do if living, and with full power, without order of court, to sell, transfer, or convey any of my property, real or personal, for the purpose of administration, division or distribution in carrying out the terms of this Will.

ARTICLE 3. DISPOSITION OF PROPERTY

3.1 Tangible Personal Property. I give all my interest in tangible personal property of every kind (for example, motor vehicles, boats, furniture, furnishings, books, objects of art, sporting equipment, jewelry, clothing and other property of a household or personal nature) as provided in a list or other writing signed by me that my Executor learns of within thirty days following appointment by the court. I give all my tangible personal property not disposed of by such a list to my Executor, if she survives me.

3.2 Residuary Estate. I give the residue of my estate to my niece, JULIA ELIZABETH WRIGHT.

ARTICLE 6. PAYMENT OF TAXES AND EXPENSES

My Executor shall pay out of the property of my residuary estate, without apportionment among the beneficiaries,

(a) all estate, inheritance and other taxes imposed by reason of my death ("estate taxes") attributable to all property subject to such taxes, including interest and penalties on those taxes, and

(b) all expenses incurred in the administration of my estate.
I have executed this Will by signing this page on _____, at CITY, STATE.

_____
SALLIE ELIZABETH WRIGHT

We, whose names are hereto signed as subscribing witnesses, have at the request of the Testatrix, _____, witnessed the execution of this Will, consisting of this page and _____(____) preceding pages, and each has signed as subscribing witness in the presence of the Testatrix and in the presence of each other on the _____day of _____

_____	_____
Witness	Address
_____	_____
Witness	Address
_____	_____
Witness	Address

AFFIDAVIT OF WITNESSES (self proving affidavit)

STATE OF _____**State**_____

COUNTY OF _____**City**_____

Each of the undersigned declares under oath on this _____day of _____, at City, State, that the following is true and correct:

(1) I am over the age of eighteen years and competent to be a witness to the WILL OF SALLIE ELIZABETH WRIGHT (the "testatrix").

(2) The testatrix in my presence and in the presence of the other witness whose signature appears below

   (a)   Declared the foregoing instrument to be her Will;
   (b)   Requested me and the other witness to act as witnesses to her Will and to make this statement; and
   (c)   Signed such instrument.

(3) I believe the testator to be of sound mind, and that in so declaring and signing, he was not acting under any duress, menace, fraud or undue influence.

(4) The other witness and I in the presence of the testator and of each other now affix our signatures as witnesses to the Will and make this statement.

[Signature]	[Signature]
Yoshiko Aoki	Andrea Granstrom
[Print Name]	[Print Name]

Residing at ____City, State____   Residing at ____City, State____

Sworn to before me this _____day of _____, 20_____.

_____
(signature and official seal)

Notary Public

REFERENCES

Additional resources are available on the LexisNexis Web Course that was created for this book.

Uniform Probate Code Article III

Andersen, *Understanding Trusts and Estates* § 2[A] (4th ed.)

Dukeminier, Johanson, Lindgren and Sitkoff, *Wills, Trusts and Estates* 33–38 (7th ed. 2005)

There are sample forms for necessary pleadings on the website that follow the UPC procedure but are not state specific, as well as links to forms to be used in particular states. The website also contains links to information on particular states' probate procedures and how to complete their forms, but not all states have comprehensive information available. The forms you use and the statutes you consult will depend on your professor's instructions.

You may want to do your own research, particularly if you are using a specifics state's laws. Often there are resources from the local bar association on probate procedure, such as practice manuals. In addition, you may find information about probate in your state on the internet.

DO NOT PROCEED TO THE NEXT PAGE UNTIL YOU HAVE COMPLETED THE EXERCISE

SELF STUDY

- How did you determine whether Sallie's estate was eligible for the informal probate procedure (if in a UPC state) or for any other unsupervised procedure in another state? Did you confirm with the state statutes that this estate was eligible?

- How did you determine whether notice to George was required? Would you give notice to George even if not required? Why?

- Did the applicable statutes require notice to creditors or just provide a shortened statute of limitations IF notice was given (this varies from state to state)? Did you think about how to give notice properly under the statute (mailing to known creditors? Publishing? If publishing, where do you publish? File notice with court?)? Look in a local newspaper where legal notices routinely are printed; you should see some notices of probate.

- In preparing the Inventory, did you include the joint tenancy bank account? This asset should not be included because it is a nonprobate asset. Julia can collect this asset by providing the bank with a death certificate.

- Are you required to file the Inventory? Why might Julia prefer not to file the Inventory with the court? Whether filed or not, even though Julia is the Personal Representative and the sole beneficiary, the Inventory is still important because it establishes the value of the assets as of Sallie's death. Julia will need to know the value at date of death for any assets that she later sells, because the date of death value is her basis for federal income tax purposes. See Internal Revenue Code § 1014. For this reason, often attorneys list nonprobate assets and their value on an inventory that will not be filed with the court, so that there is a complete record of date of death value of all the decedent's assets.

- Is there anything in the forms that you do not understand? If so, you should look up the terms, look in resources regarding probate procedure or ask the professor.

- Note that the Letters Testamentary are often issued by the Court Clerk and are not prepared by the attorney. The form is included here so that you can see what it looks like. This is a critical document. Once the Personal Representative has this document, he or she uses it to evidence her authority when dealing with third parties who hold the decedent's assets, such as banks and brokers. You can usually obtain several originals of the Letters Testamentary upon paying the necessary fees, which is helpful because some third parties may want to keep an original or may want the Personal Representative to mail an original to an out of state office.

- The Proof of Notice form is very common. Any time a notice in a court proceeding is required by law, it is either required or advisable to file with the court proof of giving such notice.

Chapter 2

INTESTACY: IDENTIFYING HEIRS

INTRODUCTION

Lawyers regularly look to forms for help in drafting documents. Often overlooked, however, are the drafting models available in various uniform statutes and the Restatements of many areas of law. Drafted (and redrafted, many times) by panels of experts, these sources can provide clearer ways of expressing familiar concepts. Because they are law reform documents, they also suggest innovative approaches that may be missing from more traditional sources of forms.

This exercise appears in conjunction with your study of intestacy statutes so it can serve two functions at once: to help you understand the structure of intestacy statutes and to give you the opportunity to practice adapting statutory language to a private document, like a will.

Depending upon the language of a statute or document, descendants might end up sharing a decedent's property an infinite number of different ways. Over time, however, common patterns have emerged. For ease of communication, we identify each of the three main patterns by a label. But be careful: these terms do not carry universally agreed upon meanings. Do not use them without defining them. Even the familiar, legal-sounding "per stirpes" means different things in different jurisdictions.

One approach (here called "strict per stirpes") is to divide the estate at the level of the decedent's children. If the child has predeceased, leaving descendants, the descendants take their parent's share ("represent" their parents), and so on down the line. A second approach also uses the notion of representation, but divides the estate at the first generation containing survivors. For example, if none of the children survived, but they left children who survived their grandparent, this scheme (here, "per capita with representation") would start dividing at the grandchildren's generation and continue from there. A third approach (here called "per capita at each generation" and now the UPC position) doesn't use representation. The estate is divided at the first generation containing survivors, but if some in that generation have died leaving descendants who survived the decedent, all the remaining shares are dumped into a pot to be re-divided under the same scheme. For graphic illustrations to help you visualize these differences, see the PowerPoint slides in the online materials.

Perhaps the most important lesson you could take away from this exercise is understanding how to use the "divide into as many equal shares as:...." device, illustrated in UPC § 2-106. It is adaptable to many different situations. The key is to create only the minimum number of shares you'll need. For example, suppose your client wanted a strict per stirpes division and had three children: Abby survived; Bill died, but his two children survived; Carol died leaving no descendants. "Create one share for each of my children" gives too many shares, because now we have one for Carol. Disposing of Carol's share requires a lot of extra language. Instead, say something like "divide my estate into as many shares as I leave: (1) children who survive me, and (2) children who do not survive me, but leave one or more descendants who survive me." Another way of stating the principle is: "Don't give property to dead people."

Keep in mind that you need to *adapt*, not copy, language. You are dealing with a will, not an intestate estate. There are two basic ways to approach dispository clauses in this context:

1. You may say [for example] "divide according to a per capita with representation scheme" **AND** also create a separate section defining the relevant term. The advantage of this approach is that you can use the same scheme in different parts of a document without redrafting each time. [Definitions usually begin with the word being defined and often set off the defined word in different type or quotation marks: "*Xxxx* means...."]

2. You may use the dispository section itself to identify precisely how to divide the estate.

Well-drafted language, like the UPC or the Restatement (Third) of Property, can help in at least two ways. It can remind you of alternative schemes you can discuss with your clients, to get them thinking. It can later serve a model from which you can craft the particular language needed. Remember: the law does not mandate that your client pick one of these approaches. They are only starting places.

SKILLS INVOLVED: Using statutory language as a model for drafting private instruments.

GENERAL DESCRIPTION OF EXERCISE: Draft language for a will's dispository clause, describing how to divide assets among a client's descendants.

PARTICIPANTS NEEDED: This is a solo exercise.

ESTIMATED TIME REQUIRED:

Task 1: 15–30 minutes

Task 2: 15–30 minutes

Task 3: 30–45 minutes

LEVEL OF DIFFICULTY (1–5):

ROLE IN EXERCISE: You represent an unmarried client who wants to divide her assets among her descendants.

THE EXERCISE

Your client is unmarried and currently has three children. She wants her will to give her property to her surviving descendants. Assume the will elsewhere defines "survive" [to add a time element] and "descendants" [to cover non-marital and adopted children]. Draft ONLY the dispository language, not the whole will.

TASK 1: Draft language necessary to divide her estate among her descendants according to a strict per stirpes scheme.

TASK 2: Draft language necessary to divide her estate among her descendants according to a per capita with representation scheme.

TASK 3: Draft language necessary to divide her estate among her descendants according to a per capita at each generation scheme.

REFERENCES

Additional resources are available on the LexisNexis Web Course that was created for this book.

Uniform Probate Code §§ 2-106; 2-709, Restatement (Third) of Property: Wills & Other Donative Transfers § 2.3, comment

Roger W. Andersen, *Understanding Trusts & Estates* § 2[A] (4th ed. 2009)

Roger W. Andersen & Ira M. Bloom, *Fundamentals of Trusts and Estates* (3d ed. 2007) pgs 73–77

PowerPoint slides available on the online platform. (Black letters indicate survivors. Colors identify the family sub-divisions that each scheme uses.)

DO NOT PROCEED TO THE NEXT PAGE UNTIL YOU HAVE COMPLETED THE EXERCISE

SELF-STUDY

- Test your drafts against the family tree in the PowerPoint slides in the online materials. (Black letters indicate survivors. Colors identify the family sub-divisions that each scheme uses.) Do you get the following shares?

    Strict per stirpes: W — 1/3. K — 1/6. O & X — 1/9 each. U & V — 1/12 each. Y & Z — 1/18 each

    Per capita with representation: K, O, W & X — 1/6 each. U, V, Y & Z — 1/12 each.

    Per capita at each generation: K & O — 1/6 each. U, V, W, X, Y & Z — 1/9 each.

- How easy was your language to apply? How might clarity be improved? Should you break the material into more sentences? Number each step in the analysis? Change the format with different paragraphing or indenting?

- Did you spell "descendants" correctly?

- Evaluate each approach as a default rule (the intestate statute). Which most closely mirrors what you believe most decedents would prefer? Which is most "fair"? If you were a legislator, would you vote for adopting one of these systems or something else? Why?

- Assume you are about to meet with an elderly client with a large family. How would you prepare to describe various options? Oral descriptions? Written handouts? Charts? PowerPoint? How would you avoid overload? How might you overcome the risk that laying out choices will limit the imagination, rather than prompt it?

SAMPLE DRAFTS

Additional resources are available on the LexisNexis Web Course that was created for this book.

Chapter 3

WILLS: COMPONENTS

INTRODUCTION

The mostly-straightforward nature of basic requirements for a will and the inaccurate term "simple will," mask subtleties that require a lawyer's careful attention. The challenges come from two directions.

First, legal doctrine can lurk in the background, so slight differences in language can create drastically different results. Precise drafting is critical.

Second, clients' desires may not be well-formed (e.g., What if a primary beneficiary becomes disabled or doesn't survive you?). The personal, "counselor" side of lawyering comes to the fore. Good lawyers treat each client as an individual, not just another in a stream who all need "standard" wills. A client's will may be one of hundreds to the lawyer, but it may be the only one the client ever has, and it reflects the reality of someone facing their own mortality.

Good lawyers recognize that both the letters they send *and* the documents they draft are devices for communicating with clients. To be efficient, lawyers use forms. Good lawyers find or develop forms that use clear language clients can understand. They then adapt the forms to fit the needs of each client. Standard "here's the draft of your will" letters include a personal touch. Clauses in the standard will form get careful review, to be sure they all apply.

Here are some guidelines to help as you identify the best forms and as you develop your own language:

- Organize the will logically. Group like things together and put them in a sensible order. Pay particular attention to hierarchy. Which topics are really sub-topics of something else? Avoid creating documents that constantly run down the left margin.

- Use headings. Articulating what's in a particular section both helps you organize and helps the reader find stuff. It's possible to use too many headings, but for starters *err on the side of adding them*. After all, you may be the poor person looking for some provision many years later.

- Use tabulation (like this list). Sometimes tabulation clarifies meaning by setting out individual items in a list in a way that makes it easy to tell where the breaks are. Often, tabulation can save repetition. To accomplish that, put all of the common elements (the words you'd otherwise be repeating) before the colon at the top and then proceed with the items in the list that differ. (As a practical matter, we often see the tabulation possibility only *after* we've drafted something and notice that we've been repeating the same language.)

- Don't try to "sound like a lawyer." We get so used to hearing (and using) awkward, redundant language that we don't even notice it. It's a constant battle to avoid things like: "In the event that…" [if] "On the condition that…" [if] "Rest, residue and remainder…" [rest] "Second day of July" [July 2] "County of Lucas" [Lucas County] "Take into consideration" [consider].

  Also, remember that saying it, doesn't make it so. You can be totally bonkers while declaring that you are "of sound mind" (or, worse, "of sound mind and memory"). Skip it. If you are worried that a client will think that your straightforward language doesn't "look like a will," use gothic type for the heading, and put the will in a heavy-paper, personalized cover with more fancy script on the outside cover.

- Format carefully. Avoid questions of integration and sloppy execution by placing page breaks so sentences run over and by keeping the testator's and the witnesses' signatures on the same page.

As you approach the project in this chapter, recall the doctrine of independent significance, which allows giving testamentary effect to information not included in the will. Clients unaware of the doctrine's limits can undermine its effectiveness, and thus open their estate plans to challenge.

SKILLS INVOLVED: Drafting client letter and will. Client relations.

GENERAL DESCRIPTION OF EXERCISE: Draft a will that includes language identifying which parts of a book collection go to different beneficiaries; draft a cover letter to the client.

PARTICIPANTS NEEDED: This can be a solo or a small-group exercise.

ESTIMATED TIME REQUIRED:

Task 1: 30–45 minutes

Task 2: 60–90 minutes

LEVEL OF DIFFICULTY (1–5):

ROLE IN EXERCISE: You represent an elderly man who wants a will.

THE EXERCISE

Your longtime client, Arthur Mercer Dixon, is an elderly man with no close relatives, but a wide variety of interests. He sold his home several years ago and moved into a spacious apartment. He loves to read and has acquired an extensive collection of books, some of which are quite valuable. He feels kinship to several different organizations and wants his will to both benefit their missions and help maintain a continuing connection to him after his death. The books are shelved around his apartment, and at a recent meeting in your office, he identified which books should go to which organizations. Your task is to draft his will to accomplish that result and to prepare a letter to accompany the draft you send him for review. Here are your notes from the meeting:

Art Dixon — will

Books as follows:

> Fiction — bed headboard & side tables — Jefferson County (Washington) Library

> Wildlife guides — bedroom bookcase surrounding window — Sierra Club, Miami, Florida Chapter

> Genealogy & farming methods — bookcase on wall in guest room — Johnson County (Iowa) Historical Society

> Camping, hiking, outdoor guides — small bookcase under guest room window — Boy Scout Troop 14, Toledo, Ohio

> Plants — left of living room fireplace — Master Gardeners of Taos, New Mexico

> Architecture — right of fireplace — School of Architecture, University of Michigan

> Cooking — Kitchen — College of Human Ecology, Kansas State University.

Balance of Estate — Shiawassee County (Michigan) Foundation

Executor — First Bank

TASK 1: Assume you've drafted the will, and draft a cover letter you'd enclose with the will draft. Your letter should reflect your long-term relationship and should use language appropriate for an educated non-lawyer.

Your project is complicated by the fact that Arthur Dixon has been a client of your firm for many years. (He and a now-deceased partner were college roommates.) You've helped him dispose of several business interests over the last five years and have noticed that he's gotten increasingly likely to change his mind. For example, while in your office, he changed the beneficiary of a group of books because he recalled some harsh remarks by the President of the local Master Gardeners group. You don't want him endangering the integrity of his gifts by moving books around with any eye to changing beneficiaries. Decide how to raise this issue in your letter.

TASK 2: Draft a will for Arthur Dixon.

REFERENCES

Additional resources are available on the LexisNexis Web Course that was created for this book.

Roger W. Andersen, *Understanding Trusts & Estates* (4th ed. 2009)

Uniform Probate Code § 2-513

DO NOT PROCEED TO THE NEXT PAGE UNTIL YOU HAVE COMPLETED THE EXERCISE

SELF-STUDY

- How would you react if you received the cover letter from someone you know pretty well? Too stiff and formal? Too casual for this context? Do you feel talked down to? Do comments about not moving books around come off as a helpful caution or a demeaning lecture? Does the letter include terms most non-lawyers would find unfamiliar? [For more insights, ask someone who is neither a law student nor a lawyer to read the letter.]

- Does the letter answer the question, "What do I do now?" [The client may be tempted to save time and money by executing the will on his own. Given the ease of messing up, that's a bad idea.]

- Does the will's structure aid its understandability? Are there enough headings, so you can easily find the section you need without reading the text?

- Compare your draft will to the sample. Are there still too many words? Have you used three when one will do? Do you know why the words you've used are there? If not, find out. Often, they aren't necessary.

- Can a non-lawyer understand the document? [Again, try it out on someone.]

- Did you clearly identify the charities? Local or national chapters? Correct names? In practice, the best ways to get the correct names of charities are to check IRS Publication 78 (available on www.irs.gov) or to ask the charity directly.

SAMPLE DOCUMENTS

Additional resources, including a sample cover letter and sample, are available on the LexisNexis Web Course that was created for this book.

Chapter 4

WILLS: EXECUTION

INTRODUCTION

Requirements for executing Wills remain very formal in our increasingly informal world, because the formalities help us distinguish a Will, intended to have tremendous effect after the death of the signer, from a mere "note to self" of things to do. Without the formalities, what may look like a Will is a document binding no one. The execution requirements vary significantly among the states, however, and adding to the confusion is the fact that most states have comity statutes, which authorize Wills validly executed under other state laws. For example, section 2-506 of the Uniform Probate Code states:

> A written will is valid if executed in compliance with Section 2-502 or 2-503 or if its execution complies with the law at the time of execution of the place where the will is executed, or of the law of the place where at the time of execution or at the time of death the testator is domiciled, has a place of abode, or is a national.

Therefore, under a comity statute like the UPC's, there would be at least four possible sets of requirements that could validate the Will: (1) the state statute in effect at time of probating the Will, (2) the law of place of execution at time of execution, (3) the law of testator's residence (or where testator has a home) at time of execution, and (4) the law of testator's residence (or where testator has a home) at time of testator's death. However, some states have no comity statutes or have much more limited comity provisions.

To be safe, an estate planning lawyer must comply with the execution requirements of the statute then in effect in the place of execution. Because it is possible that the client will move to another state that either has a limited comity statute or no comity statute, however, the lawyer should also consider following any additional requirements common in other states. Another state's laws also might apply if the client owns real property in another state. Generally, real property must be probated in the state where it is located, so if a decedent owning significant property at death was a resident of one state and owned real estate in another state, there would be a probate in the state of residence, and an ancillary probate in the state where the real property was located. The state supervising the ancillary probate would make an independent decision as to whether the Will is valid.

If multiple states are involved, to resolve the question of whether a decedent's will was properly executed, a lawyer needs first to identify the comity provisions of the state where the will is being submitted for probate. Next, the lawyer must determine all of the potential state statutes that could be used to validate the Will under the applicable comity rules. Finally, the lawyer must test the facts of execution against all possible execution statutes that could validate the Will execution.

In other words, in planning you expect the worst, and in defending an executed document you hope for the best. When supervising the execution of Wills, best practices indicate that you must do more than the minimum required by your own state's laws, in order to insure the enforceability of the Will regardless of where it might be probated. In this exercise, you will be defending the execution of a Will, so you will be looking for all possible arguments in favor of a valid execution.

This exercise requires you to analyze statutory provisions and apply them to a set of facts in order to determine whether the Will execution was valid. In law school, emphasis is usually placed on the reading of cases rather than statutes, but in the practice of law most attorneys spend much more time reading and applying statutes than reading cases. Learning to read a statute carefully is therefore a critical skill for practice.

When you analyze will execution statutes, look for the following possible characteristics of such statutes:

> -How many witnesses are required?

> -When must the witnesses sign?

> -Must the witnesses sign in the presence of the testator?

> -Must the witnesses sign in the presence of each other?

> -Must the witnesses be present together when the testator either signs the Will or acknowledges his or her signature?

> -Must the testator "publish" the Will?

State statutes vary greatly on these questions, as well as several others. Comity statutes also vary greatly. They can be as broad as the UPC statute stated above, or they can limit applicable rules to their own state law, plus the law of execution at time of execution. You must therefore read the precise language of the statute carefully and make no assumptions that once you see a comity statute it will be broad enough to cover the law you wish to apply.

SKILLS INVOLVED: Fact analysis and development, statutory research and construction, conflict of laws analysis, creative problem solving, developing litigation strategy, collaborative problem solving

GENERAL DESCRIPTION OF EXERCISE: Developing a strategy to defend a Will against a claim that the Will was not validly executed

PARTICIPANTS NEEDED: Task 1 is an individual project and Task 2 is collaborative, involving teams of 2 to 5 students

ESTIMATED TIME REQUIRED:

Task 1: One hour

Task 2: One-half hour to one hour to prepare and one to two hours for your group to meet and discuss and then summarize the discussion for the entire class, if required by professor

LEVEL OF DIFFICULTY (1–5):

ROLE IN EXERCISE: You are acting as lawyer for the estate of Hubert Hellstrom. Disappointed intestate heirs have raised the issue of whether the Will was validly executed, and you are researching the issue.

THE EXERCISE

You are an associate in the law firm representing the estate of Hubert Hellstrom. Mr. Hellstrom left a Will leaving one-half of his estate to be divided equally among four close friends, and the other half of his estate to the University he attended. Mr. Hellstrom's intestate heirs are two nephews. The two nephews, disappointed that they received nothing under Mr. Hellstrom's Will, have hired a lawyer, who has contacted your firm and raised several issues about the validity of the Will, including the issue of whether the Will was validly executed. The facts surrounding the execution are as follows:

At the time the Will was executed, Mr. Hellstrom was domiciled in State 1. He was planning a move to State 2, because his closest friends had all retired to that state. On a visit to State 2, he contacted a lawyer in State 2 about executing a new Will. He met with the lawyer, and the next day returned to the lawyer's office to execute the Will. He unfortunately was late for his appointment, and arrived during the lunch hour. The lawyer's staff had gone to lunch, and there was no one but the lawyer in the office so there was an insufficient number of witnesses. Mr. Hellstrom wanted to get it done, so he took the Will with him together with a memo from the lawyer telling him how to properly execute the Will. Mr. Hellstrom told the lawyer he was meeting with his friends for a late lunch and he would execute the Will at the restaurant and then return the executed document to the lawyer after his meal. The lawyer cautioned that the friends could not be witnesses because they were beneficiaries under the Will.

Mr. Hellstrom went to the restaurant, which was arranged as one large open room with the hostess desk at the front of the room by the door. As the hostess was seating him with his friends, he asked her to act as witness to his Will. Since business was slow at the time, the hostess agreed. According to the instruction sheet from the lawyer, he needed one more witness so he asked a woman just finishing her meal at the next table if she would serve as the other witness. She also agreed. He then told the two witnesses that this was his Will, and he signed it on the signature line on the last page. As he was signing the Will, the woman at the next table turned away to sign her credit card slip which was being handed to her by the waitress. She explained that she was in a hurry to leave, and asked to sign first. As she leaned over to Mr. Hellstrom's table to sign, the hostess walked to the front of the restaurant to seat a couple that had just walked in. As the woman at the next table was gathering her things, the hostess returned to the table. As the hostess leaned over to sign the Will, the woman at the next table said her goodbye's and headed towards the door and exited the restaurant. After his meal, Mr. Hellstrom returned to the lawyer's office with the Will, said he had followed the instructions to the letter, and departed. The next day he returned to his home in State 1.

Six months after the Will was signed, Mr. Hellstrom moved to State 2, where he was domiciled until his death three years later. Your law firm has submitted Mr. Hellstrom's Will to probate in State 2.

State 1, at all times relevant to the facts, had statutes identical to the 1990 Uniform Probate Code.

State 2, at all times relevant to the facts, had the following statutes in force:

Section 101. Execution of Wills

All wills and codicils, except as provided in section 102, to be valid, must be in writing, signed by the testator, or by some person in the testator's presence and by the testator's express direction writing the testator's name thereto, and declared by the testator to be the testator's will, and witnessed, at the testator's request, by two competent persons who signed as witnesses in the presence of the testator and in the presence of each other.

Section 102. Validity of Execution

A will is validly executed if executed in compliance with section 101, or in compliance with the law of the jurisdiction where the testator was domiciled at the time of the execution of the will or at the time of his death.

[These are modeled after actual state statutes]

TASK 1: Read all relevant statutes and write a brief memorandum on the validity of the Will execution. In the memo, identify issues regarding whether the will execution would be valid under the statutes, but you need not go into detail as to how those issues would be resolved. For example, you can raise issues about the meaning of "presence" or the doctrine of substantial compliance but you should not spend time discussing the details of how those issues would be resolved. Your focus should be on (1) whether either state's statutes cause validity problems for the will's execution, (2) which state's statutes would be applicable and (3) why.

TASK 2: Same facts as Task 1, except that the scene at the restaurant proceeded as follows. Mr. Hellstrom told the two witnesses that the document was his Will, and signed it while both of them watched. Immediately after signing, he clutched his chest and collapsed. Paramedics arrived but were unable to revive him, and as they were taking him out of the restaurant, the witnesses both signed the Will. For this Task, assume that the statute controlling whether the will execution was valid reads as follows:

(a) Except as provided in this part, a will shall be in writing and satisfy the requirements of this section.

(b) The will shall be signed by one of the following:

    (1) By the testator.

    (2) In the testator's name by some other person in the testator's presence and by the testator's direction.

(c) The will shall be witnessed by being signed by at least two persons each of whom (1) being present at the same time, witnessed either the signing of the will or the testator's acknowledgment of the signature or of the will and (2) understand that the instrument they sign is the testator's will.

Read *Casenote: Estate of Saueressig and Post-Death Subscription: The Protective Function Reborn,* 39 MCGEORGE L. REV. 359 (2008) (linked on website). Meet with the groups assigned by your professor (groups of 3 to 6 students) and discuss the likelihood that the Will would be valid, and whether it should be. For additional reference, review the current UPC provisions regarding requirements of witnessing and the comments that follow those sections.

REFERENCES

Additional resources are available on the LexisNexis Web Course that was created for this book.

Andersen, *Understanding T&E* § 7[B] (4th ed)

Jeffrey A. Schoenblum, 2006 <u>Multistate Guide to Estate Planning</u> at Table 1

This table lists the execution requirements (including the comity provisions) of the fifty states and the District of Columbia. The table identifies 16 different characteristics of execution statutes and gives each state's laws on each characteristic.

DO NOT PROCEED TO THE NEXT PAGE UNTIL YOU HAVE COMPLETED THE EXERCISE

SELF-STUDY

TASK 1:

- Did you identify the potential execution issues from the facts of the problem, based on what you know about statutory execution requirements generally? In other words, just by reading the facts, you should be able to see that if a state had a very formal execution statute that answered "yes" to most of the questions asked about these statutes in the introduction, there would be elements missing.

- Did you find and read the applicable UPC section (section 2-502) and determine exactly what was required for a valid execution under that section?

- Did you read the statutes for State 2 and compare its requirements for a valid execution? How do the two statutory schemes differ? Are there sufficient differences that the Will would clearly be valid under one statute but possibly invalid under the other?

- Did you identify the comity statute for State 2 as the one applicable to your problem, since the Will is being probated in State 2? How does the State 2 comity statute differ from the UPC comity statute?

- Under the applicable comity statute, could you apply either state's Will execution statute? Did that help your defense of the Will?

- A sample memorandum is posted on the website. Was your memorandum as short and succinct as the sample? Remember, efficiency saves the client money.

TASK 2:

- Were you able to determine that under the given statute, the timing of the witnesses' signatures was not addressed? Were the other requirements of the statute satisfied?

- Which side of the controversy on whether postmortem witness signatures are valid did you find more persuasive? Did the facts of this problem affect your choice? Are the facts of the cases discussed in the law review note more problematic? Had you made up your mind before the group discussion? Did other students' comments influence your thinking?

Chapter 5

WILLS: INTERPRETATION

INTRODUCTION

Many of the cases in your casebook could have been avoided if the lawyer preparing the Will had had better drafting skills. This exercise provides you with an opportunity to see if you can do better than those lawyers.

The key to good Will drafting (and drafting any planning document) is planning for unforeseen circumstances. The drafter of the Will does not know if the testator will die a week or three decades after a Will is executed, and cannot assume that the testator will take the trouble to update his or her Will if personal circumstances change. A competent drafter knows to ask the "what if" questions and provide in the Will for as many unexpected changes as possible. Most testators are not trained to think in terms of changed circumstances and to expect that their assets and family members will not change drastically. It is the role of the lawyer to point out these possibilities and to draft a Will that is as flexible as possible.

There are various rules of interpretation that a court will apply when an ambiguity appears or an unplanned event occurs after execution of a Will. Examples of those rules are the principles of lapse (and anti-lapse statutes) and ademption, and the limited admissibility of extrinsic evidence. However, the careful drafter does not rely on these doctrines to resolve problems of interpretation. The goal is to draft a Will that is clear on its face, without the aid of additional evidence or rules of interpretation. Any controversies ultimately may be resolved by a court, but resolving those controversies with extrinsic evidence and rules of interpretation will cost time and money. Also, the resolution may not be consistent with the testator's intent, had the testator considered all the possibilities.

Another danger is that although the Will may contain no ambiguities and may be enforceable on its face, changed circumstances result in an estate plan very different than what the testator intended. For example, when the size and nature of the testator's estate changes before the testator dies, specific gifts, which appeared relatively minor at the time the will was drafted, a much larger share of the estate than the residuary beneficiaries because the residue abates first.

One development that can occur is the change of the testator's residence. Lawyers often are only familiar with the law of Wills in their own state, and draft wills based on that law. However, if a testator changes his or her residence before death, then except for a few narrow exceptions the laws of the state of residence will apply. It is also possible for one state's laws to change between the date of execution and date of the testator's death. It is therefore critical to draft a Will that is able to cross state lines and endure the passage of time (and new statutes) and yet still result in the testator's intended distribution. Issues such as intestacy, ademption, anti-lapse and omitted spouses and children can vary greatly from state to state, and the drafter cannot assume that the statute in place at the time of execution will be applicable upon the testator's death. Consequences of changed circumstances and alternative distributions therefore need to be spelled out in the Will.

In addition to planning for the unexpected, good drafting skills also include precision and clarity. If the testator wants a complicated formula to be used in distribution, brevity should yield to clarity. Feel free to use examples and other explanations, in order to avoid ambiguities. Another trap is insufficient identification of beneficiaries. A thorough estate planner confirms all names, particularly the names of charitable organizations.

SKILLS INVOLVED: Fact analysis and development, drafting skills, creative problem solving

GENERAL DESCRIPTION OF EXERCISE: Drafting Will clauses

PARTICIPANTS NEEDED: This is an individual exercise to be completed by one student.

ESTIMATED TIME REQUIRED:

Task 1: One-half hour

Task 2: One hour

LEVEL OF DIFFICULTY (1–5):

ROLE IN EXERCISE: You are acting as lawyer for Trixie Trask, who has asked you to draft a Will for her.

THE EXERCISE

Your client, Trixie Trask, is an elderly woman with about $2 million in assets. She has come to see you to draft her Will. She would like the following provisions in her Will.

- She has two dogs that she wants to be provided for on her death. The dogs are fairly young; she wants to leave the dogs to her young neighbor Sally Hume together with $50,000 to be used for their care.

- Because of her love of animals, she would like to leave $20,000 to the Humane Society or the SPCA, or similar animal protection society. She does not care about which specific organization is named.

- Her living relatives are her sister Sheila Fordham and Sheila's two daughters, Amber Fordham and Brittany Fordham. Trixie wants to leave only some personal mementos to Sheila, and the bulk of her estate, after the gifts for the animals, to the two nieces. She favors Amber over Brittany, because Amber visits her frequently, takes her to run errands, and generally looks out for her, whereas Brittany doesn't do much more than send her a Christmas card. She wants to leave $100,000 to Brittany and the remainder of her estate to Amber. Brittany has no children but Amber is married and has a grown son. Trixie dislikes Amber's son and does not want to leave anything to him. You are concerned that Trixie may need to deplete her assets if she needs nursing home care or has other increased expenses, and that if the assets are depleted, Amber would receive a smaller share of the estate than Trixie intended. Trixie wants Amber to serve as executor of the estate.

APPLICABLE LAW: Because a Will is a portable document, you should draft the exercise assuming that any of the state laws in this area could be applicable. For Task 2, the provision for her dogs, assume that section 408 of the Uniform Trust Code (linked on the webpage) is in effect for your jurisdiction. Your professor may choose to have you use the applicable law in your state.

TASK 1: Draft the Will clause that makes the gifts to Amber and Brittany. There is a Will form on the website that you can use as a model.

TASK 2: Draft the entire Will for Trixie. There is a Will form on the website to use as a framework. There are also forms for the pet provisions.

RESOURCES

Andersen, *Understanding Trusts and Estates* § § 45 & 46 (4th ed.)

On the website there is a link to the IRS website's listing of all U.S. tax exempt charitable organizations. That list should help you with identifying the name of the beneficiary animal protection society (Task 2).

DO NOT PROCEED TO THE NEXT PAGE UNTIL YOU HAVE COMPLETED THE EXERCISE

SELF-STUDY

TASK 1:

- How did you protect Trixie's intent that Amber receive the bulk of her estate? If you drafted the clause as Trixie requested, Trixie's intent was in danger. If, for example, Trixie's estate was depleted by medical expenses down to $200,000 by the time of her death, then the bequest for her dogs would use $50,000, the gift to the Humane Society would use another $20,000, and the gift to Brittany would use $100,000, leaving only $30,000 for Amber. There are many ways to keep this from happening. One is to tie the size of the cash gifts to the size of the entire estate. Another is to include a "cut-back" provision;" in other words, add language following the cash gift that if the cash gift exceeds a certain percentage of the entire estate or exceeds a certain percentage of the residue that is going to Amber, then the cash gift is to be reduced.

- In the gift to Amber, how did you avoid the possibility that if Amber predeceased Trixie, Amber's son would be entitled to Amber's share, which is clearly not Trixie's intent. You need to provide an alternative disposition in the event that Amber predeceases and draft so that any applicable anti-lapse statute would not take effect.

TASK 2:

- Did you use the pet trust format for the gift of $50,000 to care for the dogs? Or did you just give the cash outright to the neighbor? If you used the trust format, did you provide for distribution of the remainder of the trust funds if the dogs died before all of the funds were spent?

- How did you identify the Humane Society or SPCA in the Will? Like many national charities, there are regional and local branches of such groups that are separate organizations. You should have selected a suitable organization from the IRS listing (after consulting with your client, of course!).

- Did you require survivorship for all of the gifts, and provide instructions as to what is to be done with a gift if the beneficiary does not survive? Did you give alternate provisions if the animal protection society you specified was no longer in existence?

- How did you handle the gift of mementos to Sheila? Did you rely on the list of tangible personal property clause or put a specific provision in the Will?

- Did you give reasons in the Will for the distribution plan, that is, did you put in language that Trixie does not like Amber's son, or that Brittany has not done enough for her? That type of language is generally not a good idea, for two primary reasons. First, it may give Brittany a means to contest the will, if she had evidence that she in fact had done as much as Amber for Trixie. Second, because Wills are public documents once the testator has died, any negative statements about family members in the Will could give the maligned family members the right to sue for defamation.

Chapter 6

WILLS: CAPACITY AND UNDUE INFLUENCE (PLANNING)

INTRODUCTION

This chapter requires that you apply what you know about challenges to Wills based on lack of the testator's capacity or undue influence to the planning process. You have seen in the cases you have read for class that lack of testamentary capacity and undue influence are common challenges to Wills brought by disappointed heirs after the death of the testator. We address in another chapter how to successfully assert or defend against such claims, but in this chapter we address a critical and often overlooked task for the estate planner (or for any lawyer who is involved in the planning stage of a transaction). That task is avoiding future litigation, or at least lessening its likelihood of success.

When a lawyer is retained to prepare a client's Will or other estate planning documents, the lawyer is ethically required to do a competent job. Merely putting down on paper what the client wishes does not satisfy competence. The lawyer must also apply his or her professional skill and judgment to draft a document that not only says what the client wants it to say, but that also has a reasonable probability of being effective in carrying out the client's wishes. For example, if a client asks that a lawyer include a provision that the lawyer knows will not be enforced, a competent lawyer would advise the client that such a provision will not achieve the client's objective, and would work with the client to come up with an alternative method of carrying out the client's wishes if possible.

A competent estate planner also has to be concerned about potential challenges to the client's estate plan after the client has died. This is particularly critical because the client will not be available to defend against the allegations. While this can be a difficult conversation with a client, the estate planning attorney must raise the issue of potential challenges with the client and must try to (a) draft the estate plan to be as challenge-proof as possible; and (b) collect evidence as to the client's intentions and the circumstances of the will planning and execution to be used to defend against any challenges brought at the death of the client.

In this exercise, you have the circumstance of a client who is very old (albeit very active and capable) and who is leaving her estate to charity instead of to her younger relatives. It is a sad reality that ageism exists and that a person in their nineties is likely to be perceived as less than competent just by virtue of their age. When you add the client's advanced age to the likely disappointment of the younger family members, your job as estate planner now includes not only preparing the Will but also protecting against an unwarranted attack by the disappointed heirs when the client dies.

This problem also raises an ethical issue that commonly arises with estate planners. The client in the exercise has asked you to name yourself in the Will to serve as personal representative. Is this a conflict of interest?

SKILLS INVOLVED: Fact analysis and development, drafting skills, creative problem solving, ethical problem solving.

GENERAL DESCRIPTION OF EXERCISE: Preparation of letter to client whose estate plan is likely to face challenges regarding capacity and undue influence.

PARTICIPANTS NEEDED: This is an individual exercise to be completed by one student.

ESTIMATED TIME REQUIRED:

One hour

LEVEL OF DIFFICULTY (1–5):

ROLE IN EXERCISE: You are acting as lawyer for Andrea Esterhaus, an elderly woman who has asked you to prepare her will.

APPLICABLE LAW: Assume that the cases in your casebook on testamentary capacity and undue influence were decided in your jurisdiction. Your professor may also ask that you research case law on these issues in a particular jurisdiction.

In addressing the issue of naming yourself as personal representative, review RPC 1.7 and 1.8, and the ACTEC commentaries on those rules. A link to the ACTEC commentaries is on the website.

THE EXERCISE

Andrea Esterhaus is a 92 year old woman who lives in her own apartment in a downtown retirement complex. She was never married and never had children. She comes from a very poor, rural background. When she graduated from high school, she went to work as a secretary for the State Department, and worked there until her retirement. She took many job assignments in overseas locations and was able to travel all over the world. She was an active hiker and mountain climber and still hikes on the weekends with a local hiking club. At all of her appointments with you, she is very well-groomed and her clothes are simple and appear to be a bit worn but very high quality. She is very tiny and frail in appearance, although she moves well and says that she walks the twenty blocks from her apartment to your office.

She has asked you to prepare her Will. Her current assets consist of her own savings of $750,000, the contents of her apartment, (which include artwork and crafts that she collected on her world travels), and a separate account with a brokerage firm with a current value of $2 million. The $2 million was her share of her brother's estate. Her brother never graduated high school and went to work at the local factory when he was a teenager. He was horribly injured in an explosion at the factory, leaving him an invalid. He was paid a large settlement as a result of litigation following the explosion, but died shortly after the settlement was paid. Andrea and her sister Cecile were his only surviving heirs, so they inherited the remainder of the settlement. Andrea has never spent any of her share, but instead continues to invest it. She would like to leave these funds to the high school in her home town, in memory of her brother, with the request that the school use the funds for programs to help students like her brother stay in school. She has a list of the items in her apartment and the different friends from the hiking club she would like to receive these items. As for her remaining funds, she would like those divided equally between the local food bank and the hiking club's foundation that provides wilderness adventures to underprivileged youth.

She says that her only living relatives are her two grandnieces, Morgan and Brittany. Her sister Cecile is now deceased. Cecile had one son, Albert, who was the father of Morgan and Brittany, and he died of a heart attack at age 50. Andrea tells you that Cecile used her share of their brother's estate to purchase a large home in the suburbs, and because her husband was successful, left a "decent" inheritance for Albert and his daughters. Andrea said that she never was comfortable with her sister's lavish lifestyle and has always thought that Albert and his daughters were somewhat spoiled and materialistic. Morgan and Brittany stay in touch with Andrea, coming to see her occasionally and inviting her to their homes for holidays. Andrea says that she likes them well enough, but says that they are boring. They are both married with good jobs but seem interested only in material possessions and their circle of friends and never seem interested in the outside world. She suspects that they stay in touch with her only to ensure that they will inherit her estate. She has never made representations to them that she was going to leave them anything, but they ask questions about her finances, comment often about the inheritance from Andrea's brother, and Brittany told Andrea recently that "it's OK with me if you want to give some of this stuff in your apartment to your friends, because it's not really my style. Except anything that's really valuable, of course." Andrea did not say anything, and did not correct Brittany's apparent assumption that she would be inheriting Andrea's property.

Andrea explains that she does not want to leave out her grandnieces out of anger or dislike. Instead, she has held onto the money from her brother's estate always with the intention that she would use the funds to do something to honor his life and memory. As for her own property, she sees that her nieces are financially comfortable and have already benefited from their grandmother's and father's estates, and she has never forgotten how hard her impoverished childhood was. She would therefore prefer to leave her money in ways that benefit people who lack resources.

Finally, she asks that you name yourself to act as executor to her Will. She explains that she has no one else.

Draft a letter to Andrea that discusses the issue of a potential challenge to her Will by her nieces on the grounds that she lacked testamentary capacity, and your proposed strategies to protect her estate plan from such a challenge. Also address in the letter the issue of whether you can name yourself as personal representative.

RESOURCES

Additional resources are available on the LexisNexis Web Course that was created for this book.

Andersen, *Understanding Trusts and Estates* § 7[A] (4th ed.)

**DO NOT PROCEED TO THE NEXT PAGE UNTIL YOU HAVE
COMPLETED THE EXERCISE**

SELF STUDY

1. Your first concern should be how to bring up the issue with Andrea sensitively, because an elderly client, particularly one so active and independent, will resent any suggestion that merely because of her age her competence is suspect. She may also resent the suggestion that her nieces might allege that her friends at the hiking group influenced her decision to set up the fund with the hiking foundation. Usually, you would have raised these issues with her in person at your meeting, because in a face to face conversation you can allow her to react to the possibility of someone challenging her competence and reassure her about your own views. On the other hand, you have to be realistic with her about the potential for a challenge, even though this is a difficult conversation. Your language in the letter stating the problem therefore must be diplomatic yet realistic.

2. There are any number of strategies available to make a good record now as to Andrea's capacity. One controversial strategy is to videotape the will execution ceremony, and include a conversation between the lawyer and the testator to allow the testator to explain the estate plan and the reasons behind it in his or her own words. This technique is controversial because it can often backfire if the testator, even though mentally competent, is in frail health or becomes nervous in front of the camera. Also, you need to be cautious about the testator being too negative and perhaps embellishing the reasons why certain persons are being disinherited. It may be something you would want to raise with the client as a possibility, but you need to discuss the pros and cons of videotaping, again being careful to be diplomatic. Unless the client raises the idea, if the attorney's own observations indicate that the client would not make a strong appearance on tape, the attorney can choose not to suggest this option.

3. Because the most likely challenge will be to her testamentary capacity, an excellent way to refute a later allegation of incompetence would be for Andrea to have her attending physician do a general competency exam and make that exam part of her medical records. There is a risk that if the physician's findings are not altogether positive, that exam would nevertheless be discoverable as part of her medical records. Also, the test of testamentary capacity is a legal one and is not the same as a medical exam for mental competence. Testamentary capacity is a very low standard; a person can have impaired

capacity to carry out the ordinary tasks of daily life but may still have testamentary capacity. You should therefore follow through with this technique only if you are confident that the exam report will be positive.

4. If you decide against a video, a written statement from Andrea as to why she is leaving her property in this way should be considered. It is usually not advisable to put language in the Will because the lawyer is the drafter of the Will, and any negative comments about family members could be a basis for a defamation claim by the maligned family member. A written statement by Andrea should be kept on a positive note, explaining her motives for using her money to honor her brother and help the disadvantaged, rather than criticizing her nieces.

5. There are many other techniques for avoiding will contests that you may have considered. These include: using a revocable living trust instead of a Will (because some consider RLTs to be harder to contest than Wills), no contest (in terrorem) clauses in the Will, and using lifetime transfers. For example, it might be advisable for Andrea to make the gift of her brother's settlement money to the high school now, particularly since she does not intend to spend the money during her lifetime. One advantage of this would be that she could see the money put to work and have some involvement and input into setting up the scholarship program. One disadvantage would be that if she had a financial crisis, such as a health care need, she would not have those funds to access. As for no contest clauses, in order for those to be effective you need to "bait the trap." In other words, there would have to be some gift to the nieces that they would lose if they challenged the Will. Another drafting technique when you are concerned about a will contest is drafting to affect the parties' standing to bring a challenge. The nieces' standing to challenge the Will would be based on their status of intestate heirs, but the Will drafter can insert another party that would be an alternate taker. So for example, if there was concern that the nieces would allege the hiking group unduly influenced Andrea to give money to the foundation, the Will could provide that if that gift were invalidated, then the gift would go instead to some other organization with which Andrea had no lifetime contact (and therefore no opportunity for undue influence) and which would be sympathetic to the goal of setting up a fund with the hiking foundation and therefore not likely to challenge it. Thus, in order for the nieces to have standing to raise the undue

influence claim they would also need grounds to challenge the gift to the alternate organization.

6. This exercise is about using your creativity to help Andrea carry out her intentions. Any ideas that you had in addition to those listed here are not any less worthwhile and show that you understood the purpose of the exercise.

7. There are links to articles on the website that discuss how to plan for potential will contests and may give you further ideas.

8. You may have included in your letter a discussion of how to dispose of the personal items in her apartment and the availability (in most states) of incorporation by reference in the Will of a list that she can prepare herself.

9. As for the issue of serving as personal representative, according to the ACTEC guidelines, this is acceptable only if Andrea is given full disclosure of the consequences of your serving. Your letter should therefore include details about the role of a personal representative, how a layperson could also fill that role and how you would likely be more expensive than a layperson executor. Also, you should note from the Commentaries whether your state has special rules on this issue (e.g., California).

Chapter 7

WILLS: CAPACITY AND UNDUE INFLUENCE (NEGOTIATION)

INTRODUCTION

The flexibility of the testamentary capacity and undue influence doctrines allows outraged, disappointed or blatantly greedy relatives to challenge wills that would deny them what they claim is their "fair share" of an estate. Lack of capacity would invalidate the whole document. Undue influence could invalidate the whole document or only those provisions resulting from the influence. Recall that only those who would benefit from a finding of invalidity would have standing to challenge. Whatever their initial reactions, disinherited individuals soon realize that hiring a lawyer can be costly, and that litigation is especially so. An overwhelming percentage of potential claims are resolved by alternative dispute resolution.

This exercise gives you the opportunity to "get inside" a negotiation from a particular perspective. The better able you are to adopt your role, the better you will see and — perhaps more importantly — feel what negotiations can be like. Later, when you step back out of your role, you can contribute to and learn from a discussion of what all participants learned.

There is a great deal of theory about the dynamics of the negotiation process. While you would benefit from exploring that material, it is beyond the scope of this single exercise to attempt more than an experiential introduction. The following questions, however, should stimulate your thinking about how to approach the exercise.

- What are your (or your client's) various interests in the litigation and in a possible settlement, other than the obvious financial ones?

- You have, or may have, long-term relationships with the other lawyers involved in this case. How can you protect those relationships without undermining your client's best interests?

- What informal discovery should be done (or avoided) prior to the settlement meeting?

- What does each party have at risk if the case goes to trial? Which parties are in an all-or-nothing position if there is a judicial determination as to the validity of the will?

- What are the true ranges of acceptable settlement for each party after taking into consideration avoidance of expenses?

- What costs other than fees and litigation expenses can be avoided or minimized by reaching consensus rather than trying the case?

- How can you advocate effectively for your client while seeking resolution by settlement?

SKILLS INVOLVED: Fact analysis, counseling, negotiation.

GENERAL DESCRIPTION OF EXERCISE: Negotiate among a variety of persons over the possibility of a will contest.

PARTICIPANTS NEEDED: Teams of 8 (or 9) persons.

ESTIMATED TIME REQUIRED:

4–6 hours

LEVEL OF DIFFICULTY (1–5):

ROLE IN EXERCISE: You will be either one of the parties to a potential will contest or one of the lawyers involved.

BASIC FACTS (AVAILABLE TO ALL PARTICIPANTS)

Otterbein Dressler died three months ago, at the age of 71 years. Two years earlier, he executed a will standard in most respects. It includes a clause that would invalidate "all gifts to any person or organization that contests this will." No other wills have surfaced and if this one is set aside, Dressler will have died intestate. If the will is admitted to probate and not contested, it would result in the following dispositions:

1. Daugherty: $5,000
2. Moore: $10,000
3. Henry Moore (Moore's son): $10,000
4. Gifts to a variety of friends, totaling: $15,000
5. Mabel Meeks (housekeeper): $25,000
6. Sanderson: $100,000
7. Otis: $650,000
8. The Society: Residue

Dressler's probate estate is estimated to be about $1,250,000. He had no significant debts.

The will was prepared by Quinn, a longtime friend of Dressler, and a member of the local board of The Saving Graces Society (hereafter "Society"). Quinn is named the Executor under the will and is also entitled to act as attorney for the estate, to charge separate fees in each capacity, and to not have to post bond. Quinn's law partner, Chris Conklin, will be the attorney for the Society in these negotiations.

Surviving Dressler as his closest living relatives are three siblings: Sanderson, Moore, and Daugherty.

Otterbein Dressler never married nor had children. He toiled as a farmer, spent little and acquired parcels of farmland as he saved money. He never believed in borrowing. At his death, he owned over 2,000 acres of prime farmland as well as a modern home, several modern barns and excellent farm equipment. All of the real estate is located in the state of his domicile at death. He also had over $100,000 in bank accounts in his name alone.

Dressler was a religious person throughout his lifetime, but never fanatical or preachy. About ten years ago, he attended several meetings of the Society, and the next year he became a member. The Society is an unaffiliated national religious organization devoted to providing social services in a wide variety contexts. From then until his death, he regularly attended monthly meetings and donated annually to its purposes, ranging from a high of $3,500 in one year to a low of $800 in another year, until this year when he made a gift of $50,000. He rarely made charitable gifts to any other cause.

Until about two years ago, Dressler had a warm relationship with two of his siblings, Sanderson and Moore, as well as with most of his nieces and nephews. Although he never made especially generous gifts to any of them, he always gave them something on holidays and birthdays, and had made loans to several of the relatives over the years. From youth, his relationship with Daugherty had been rocky — not because of any one incident creating dislike (so far as anyone knew) but just because they were both strong-willed and rubbed each other the wrong way much of the time.

Four years ago, Dressler met Robin Otis, then 52 years old, at a Society meeting. According to stories several people heard and from what Otis apparently told Mr. Dressler, Otis was a reformed alcoholic who had found stability and moral sustenance while volunteering for the Society. Otis related stories about how the drinking "habit" had ruined a marriage, alienated children, and affected Otis's health. At the time they met, Otis worked as a substitute school bus driver and part-time security officer at a local bank.

After several long conversations at Society meetings, Dressler and Otis began meeting for lunches and dinners. Three years ago, they traveled together to Canada (the first time Dressler had ever been out of the country). Later that year, Otis moved into Dressler's house and lived there until the latter's death (and still lives there). (Dressler's housekeeper, Mabel Meeks, was a day housekeeper, not a live-in.)

Two years ago, Dressler suffered a mild stroke and was hospitalized for twenty days and then moved to a nursing facility. Always a robust, active and independent person, Dressler regained some strength by early October and insisted on returning home. From that time until his death he remained home, tended to by Otis and Meeks, both of whom kept all visits, except those by Quinn, to a small number and brief duration. His siblings probably only visited him about five times each between the time he returned home and his death, and none of their conversations had much depth. There was no overt animosity in these meetings, but, of course, Dressler was not the person he once was.

The will was executed two years ago, shortly after Dressler had returned home from the nursing facility. The execution ceremony was conducted by Quinn, who arranged for three witnesses, two neighbors and a day nurse, and a notary. None of the three witnesses are beneficiaries under the will. All three chatted with Dressler before the ceremony and felt, while "not the Otterbein Dressler of yesteryear" (the day nurse knew him from before his illness), he was certainly lucid. The will includes a self-proving affidavit. No beneficiary under the will was present at the execution.

Dressler's home was a county seat city of approximately 35,000 people, located about 200 miles from a major metropolitan area. The facts do not recite whether the will has yet been offered for probate and there are no obvious reasons why it must have been for these negotiations to proceed; however, a group that wants to know definitively whether it has or has not yet been offered for probate is welcome to settle that as an "agreed fact."

THE EXERCISE

You are either one of the parties to a potential will contest or one of the lawyers involved in a negotiation to try to settle the issue. The negotiation proceeds as follows:

1. Under procedures established by the professor, the class is divided into groups of eight (or nine) and each student acquires a role (described below).

2. When everyone in the group has a role, each receives a *confidential* memo giving additional facts known (initially, at least) only to that person or others who also participated in various events. Client-attorney meetings should be held as soon as possible thereafter.

3. In the discretion of the participants, various optional meetings may occur before final settlement negotiations. Some possibilities: (1) attorneys for the three siblings, (2) attorneys for Otis and the Society, (3) the siblings themselves, with or without their attorneys, (4) Olsen and Williams, with or without their attorneys present. **Note:** clients who propose to meet each other should tell their respective attorneys of their desire to do so and at least be willing to listen to their attorneys' recommendations. These meetings (if they take place) may be for fact—gathering, "feeling out," or development of joint strategies. (In groups with nine, Quinn may be at the Olsen-Williams meeting if acceptable to Thomas, Conklin and Quinn). Until the entire problem is completed by every student in the class, no student may discuss the problem or any facts they have learned with any other student from another negotiating group.

4. Settlement negotiations take place in which the parties attempt to negotiate a settlement that will avoid the possibility of a public will contest. (See guidelines below.)

5. Students shed their respective roles and discuss the process. (See self-study section below.)

THE PLAYERS

1. Mildred/Michael Sanderson — Testator's youngest sibling, age 64.

2. Kyle Kendrick — Sanderson's attorney (practices locally).

3. Carl/Clarisse Moore (age 74) or Oscar/Opal Daugherty (age 68) — Testator's other siblings. Participant may choose to play either or both roles, but must make clear which role is being played at any given time.

4. Norma/Norman Skinner — Moore's and Daugherty's attorney (one of the most prominent in the area).

5. Robin Otis —Testator's friend.

6. Sandy Thomas — Otis's attorney (senior partner in a large urban law firm).

7. Winston/Wilma Williams — Regional Director (from nearby large urban area) of The Saving Graces Society (Society).

8. Chris Conklin, attorney for the Society and law partner to Quinn.

9. [If included] Thelma/Thomas Quinn — Attorney who drew will and its named executor.

SETTLEMENT NEGOTIATION GUIDELINES

1. The exercise contemplates a face-to-face meeting among the participants so that body language, tone of voice, and close proximity can provide a more complete experience. Online alternatives should strive to re-create that sort of setting as much as possible.

2. By mutual agreement, establish a time limit between one and two hours. The time can be extended later, but only if all parties agree to a new limit. A successful conclusion ("settlement") to the negotiations is not necessary.

3. The negotiation may be conducted with all eight (or nine) persons at the table throughout, or with just the attorneys throughout. It may be started with all eight (nine), with the clients leaving part way through, or it may start with just the attorneys to be joined by the clients after the attorneys have reached an impasse or a tentative settlement. The most realistic scenario is probably attorneys-only for at least some of the time.

4. Breaks for coffee, rest stops, or whatever, are permissible, as are periodic consultations between attorneys and clients during any part of the session where the clients are not in the negotiating room.

REFERENCES

Additional resources are available on the LexisNexis Web Course that was created for this book.

Rules of Professional Conduct § § 1.6, 1.7, 1.16 and 3.7

Roger W. Andersen, *Understanding Trusts & Estates* § 7[A] (4th ed. 2009)

Jonathan G. Blattmachr, *Reducing Estate and Trust Litigation Through Disclosure, In Terrorem Clauses, Mediation and Arbitration*, 9 Cardozo J. Conflict Resol. 237 (2008)

Paul C. Giannelli, *Understanding Evidence* (2d ed. 2006)

http://www.abanet.org/litigation/ethics/settlementnegotiations.pdf

**DO NOT PROCEED TO THE NEXT PAGE UNTIL YOU HAVE
COMPLETED THE EXERCISE**

SELF-STUDY

Here are some topics for the discussion following the negotiation session:

- Did you (or your client) truly understand the general risks inherent in litigation, as well as the specific ones related to his or her position as it relates to the facts of the case?

- Do you believe the case "should" be settled rather than tried?

- What other party alliances might have been explored prior to and during the negotiations? For example, did the Society and one or more siblings ally against Otis?

- If no settlement was reached, what could you have done differently? What solutions can you identify now that might have contributed to settlement? For example, did anyone propose that the will be deemed invalid and the siblings make charitable contributions to the Society?

- If a settlement was reached, how did each client fare? Why?

Chapter 8

NONPROBATE TRANSFERS

INTRODUCTION

Increasingly, the focus of transferring property at death is shifting from the use of Wills to the use of nonprobate transfers. This trend began late in the 20th century and continues to gain speed. See John H. Langbein, *The Nonprobate Revolution and the Future of the Law of Succession*, 97 HARV. L. REV. 1108 (1984). Professor Langbein identified four common types of nonprobate transfers: retirement assets, life insurance, joint accounts and revocable living trusts. The forms of nonprobate assets are growing: we now have transfer on death beneficiary designations for stock and other securities (see Uniform Transfer on Death Security Registration Act), the broad authorization for contractual nonprobate arrangements under Uniform Probate Code section 6-101, and the emerging transfer on death deed (see Susan N. Gary, *Transfer-On-Death Deeds: The Nonprobate Revolution Continues*, 41 REAL PROP. PROB. & TR. J. 529 (2006)).

The revocable living trust is used as a true Will substitute to avoid probate, facilitate disability planning and protect privacy, among other reasons. By contrast, most of the other nonprobate assets, such as life insurance and retirement assets, are found in clients' estates even though their estate planning document of choice is a will. In fact, a retirement account can be one of the most significant of a client's assets and yet, because that type of asset is disposed of by beneficiary designation, it is not normally affected by the terms of the client's Will.

The result is that the job of the estate planner has become much more complicated. The estate planner can no longer focus on the terms of the Will. In order to carry out the client's wishes regarding his or her property, the estate planner must coordinate all of the various nonprobate assets held by the client. It is therefore critical to ask the client about any nonprobate assets and to make recommendations and assist the client in making appropriate beneficiary designations for those assets that will fit with the estate planning done in the Will.

Retirement assets in particular have complicated the estate planning task, because beneficiary designations for those assets have to take into account income tax considerations and restrictions and regulations arising from the federal laws that govern retirement assets.

Those factors are beyond the scope of a Wills and Trusts survey course, but you should know that a competent estate planner must be knowledgeable in this area in order to create a serviceable estate plan for any client.

This exercise focuses on coordination of nonprobate and probate assets just from the nontax aspect of getting the property where the client wants it to go, so it uses life insurance and joint tenancy bank accounts as the nonprobate assets at issue, which do not carry much additional regulation. However, even with those assets, statutes other than the probate statutes affect their disposition so there is some coordination of different areas of law required to perform the exercise. For example, many states will exempt the proceeds of a life insurance policy from the claims of the deceased insured's creditors. The problem sets forth a Wyoming statute that is typical for state statutes governing life insurance policies, but your professor may direct you to apply the state statute from another state or direct you to research what statutory authority exists in a certain state on this issue.

SKILLS INVOLVED: Writing skills, communications with clients, statutory research and application

GENERAL DESCRIPTION OF EXERCISE: Correspondence to client about coordinating nonprobate assets with entire estate plan

PARTICIPANTS NEEDED: This is an individual exercise

ESTIMATED TIME REQUIRED:

Task 1: One-half hour

Task 2: One-half hour

LEVEL OF DIFFICULTY (1–5):

ROLE(S) IN EXERCISE:

Task 1: You are preparing an estate plan for a married couple who have significant life insurance policies on the lives of each spouse. Your task is to advise the clients regarding disposition of the life insurance policy.

Task 2: You are representing the estate of a decedent who left a Will, a residence, and a joint tenancy bank account. Your task is to advise the executor about handling the joint tenancy bank account.

THE EXERCISE

TASK 1: You have been hired by Sylvia and Jorge Sanchez to prepare their Wills. Sylvia and Jorge have two children, Andrea and Milo, ages 7 and 5. They have requested that their Wills provide that upon the first spouse's death, the surviving spouse would be the sole beneficiary of the first spouse's estate, and on the second spouse's death, their assets would be placed in trust for the two children until the children reach the age of 30. Jorge's sister Esther is to be named trustee of the trust for the children. In response to your questions at the first meeting, they have told you that they own two life insurance policies, one on the life of each spouse, in the amount of $500,000 per policy. They also told you that they think the current beneficiary designations for the policies specify that the surviving spouse would be the sole beneficiary, and there is no contingent beneficiary named. Disregard all estate tax issues. Review the relevant sections of the UPC, and the Wyoming statute set forth below, and write your clients a letter advising them as to how they should designate beneficiaries of the life insurance policies, and why.

APPLICABLE LAW:

Uniform Probate Code

Wyo. Stat. 26-15-129:

> If a policy of insurance is executed by any person on his own life or on another life, in favor of a person other than himself, or except in cases of transfer with intent to defraud creditors, if a policy of life insurance is assigned or in any way made payable to that person, the lawful beneficiary or assignee thereof, other than the insured or the person executing insurance or executors or administrators of the insured or the person executing the insurance, are entitled to its proceeds, including death benefits, cash surrender and loan values, premiums waived and dividends, whether used in reduction of premiums or otherwise, excepting only where the debtor, subsequent to issuance of the policy, has actually elected to receive the dividends in cash, against the creditors and representatives of the insured and of the person executing the policy, and are not liable to be applied by any legal or equitable process to pay any debt or liability of the insured individual or his beneficiary or of any other person having a right under the policy, whether or not:

>> (i) The right to change the beneficiary is reserved or permitted; and

>> (ii) The policy is made payable to the person whose life is insured if the beneficiary or assignee predeceases that person, and the proceeds are exempt from all liability for any debt of the beneficiary existing at the time the policy is made available for his use.

> (b) However, subject to the statute of limitations, the amount of any premiums paid for insurance with intent to defraud creditors, with interest thereon, shall inure to

their benefit from the policy proceeds; but the insurer issuing the policy is discharged of all liability thereon by payment of its proceeds in accordance with its terms, unless before payment the insurer receives written notice at its home office, by or in behalf of a creditor of:

(i) A claim to recover for transfer made or premiums paid with intent to defraud creditors;

(ii) The amount claimed along with facts as will assist the insurer to ascertain the particular policy.

(c) For the purposes of subsections (a) and (b) of this section, a policy is payable to a person other than the insured if and to the extent that a facility-of-payment clause or similar clause in the policy permits the insurer to discharge its obligation after the death of the individual insured by paying the death benefits to a person as permitted by the clause.

NOTE: YOUR PROFESSOR MAY ASSIGN YOU A DIFFERENT STATE'S STATUTE TO APPLY TO THE FACTS OF THE PROBLEM.

TASK 2: You have been hired by Sylvia to represent her as Personal Representative of her mother's estate. Sylvia tells you that her mother died owning a residence held in her mother's name alone as well as a bank account holding $90,000. Her mother's Will leaves everything to Sylvia and her brother Abner in equal shares. Sylvia also tells you that the bank account was held in the name of her mother and Sylvia as joint tenants with right of survivorship. Sylvia's mother had added Sylvia's name to the account because Sylvia was helping her mother out by paying her bills. Sylvia has asked you whether she can just give her brother one-half of the bank account. Review the provisions of the UPC (see in particular section 6-212 and Article 2 Part 11) and write her a letter advising her how to handle the joint bank account. Would your answer be different if instead of the UPC provision, Cal. Probate Code section 5302 (linked on the website) applied?

RESOURCES

Additional resources are available on the LexisNexis Web Course that was created for this book.

Andersen, *Understanding Trusts & Estates* §§ 18, 19 & 21 (4th ed.)

DO NOT PROCEED TO THE NEXT PAGE UNTIL YOU HAVE COMPLETED THE EXERCISE

SELF STUDY

TASK 1:

(A sample letter is found on the website.)

- Did you recommend that they keep each other as primary beneficiaries, since that is consistent with the plan set forth in the Wills?

- Did you recommend a contingent beneficiary? If there is no contingent beneficiary, where would the proceeds go? To their estate? If payable to the estate, how would they be distributed? Any down sides to having the proceeds payable to the estate? Would that subject the proceeds to creditor claims in their estates? Note that it is critical for you to advise them to take advantage of any possible creditor exemption statutes, or you may be subject to a later malpractice claim. Also note that even though the state in which you are located does not protect insurance proceeds payable on death from claims of the insured's creditors, the clients may later move to a state where such protection exists. Some states protect insurance proceeds that are payable to the estate of the insured, but some states only protect the proceeds if payable to a beneficiary other than the estate. It is therefore poor advice to suggest naming the estate as beneficiary or to suggest that a contingent beneficiary is not necessary.

- If the estate is not a good contingent beneficiary, who should be named? The children are too young to be named directly. Did you recommend that Esther, as trustee for the two children, be named as the contingent beneficiary? For minor children, it is preferable to name the trust under the parents' Wills as the beneficiary rather than the children directly. If the children are named directly, and they are minors at the time the proceeds are to be paid, the insurance company will require a guardianship, conservatorship, or perhaps a Uniform Transfers to Minors custodianship if allowed under state law. Those procedures may be costly and time consuming, and the funds would be payable to the children when they were 18, rather than the age of 30 chosen by the clients.

TASK 2:

(A sample letter is posted on the website)

- Did you explain that under the UPC provision, the funds now belong entirely to Sylvia regardless of her mother's intent and the terms of the Will?

- Did you explain that if she transferred one-half to her brother, that would be considered a taxable gift?

- Did you recommend that she disclaim her interest as joint tenant, allowing the funds to flow to the estate and be distributed under the Will? How did you recommend she disclaim, in order to keep one-half? This is actually a tricky question, complicated by federal tax rules on what constitutes a valid disclaimer. There are materials on the website on this issue if you are interested. Because of these complications, estate planners discourage their clients from holding assets in joint tenancy.

- Did you find the California statute more helpful in this situation? Did you understand that language in the California statute gives you an alternative to the disclaimer approach, that avoids the complications discussed above?

Chapter 9

FAMILY PROTECTION

INTRODUCTION

One exception to testamentary freedom is the required support for surviving spouses and children. One of the most effective ways to learn the nature and extent of those protections is to negotiate a contract that waives some or all of those protections in consideration of other financial protections.

One may assume that prenuptial agreements are primarily a concern of family law attorneys. However, estate planning attorneys are just as likely to represent clients who are considering marriage and want to enter into a prenuptial agreement. Prenuptial agreements involve rights in a spouse's property at the end of a marriage, either by death or by divorce, so the issues involved are within the estate planner's expertise. Estate planners obviously work with spouses' rights at death, but also must understand potential claims by spouses at the dissolution of a marriage in order to plan a married person's estate and advise on the titling of property.

SKILLS INVOLVED: Fact analysis and development, interview skills, negotiation skills, application of legal doctrine and statutory law to client goals, drafting skills

GENERAL DESCRIPTION OF EXERCISE: Negotiate and prepare a prenuptial agreement

PARTICIPANTS NEEDED:

Task 1: One student

Task 2: This is a group exercise. It can be done with four students: two students playing the clients and two students playing the attorneys. It can also be done with two students, playing the attorneys. With only two students, the participants will negotiate and draft based only on the written fact patterns and will not be able to interview the clients for initial fact gathering or work with clients in the negotiation.

ESTIMATED TIME REQUIRED:

Task 1: One hour

Task 2: Two hours (or longer depending on the length of the negotiation)

LEVEL OF DIFFICULTY (1–5):

THE EXERCISE

Howard and Mia are engaged to be married. Howard owns and operates a small neighborhood shoe repair shop started by his grandfather and run by Howard's father until his father died seven years ago. He met Mia, a reporter for a local television station, when she did a story on struggling neighborhood businesses. Mia and Howard dated for two years, and Howard moved into Mia's house about a year ago. The house was a gift to Mia from her parents. Howard likes home improvement projects and does all the home repairs. Since he's been living there, he put in a new driveway and turned the unfinished basement into a study and home movie theater.

Howard's shoe repair shop is indeed struggling. In fact, in the last year, it was barely breaking even, even with Howard taking minimal pay. A few times, Mia had to give him money to cover his ever increasing rent. Howard is very reluctant to close the shop, however, because it bears his grandfather's name and because his father devoted his whole life to the shop and being part of the neighborhood.

APPLICABLE LAW: The exercise may be set geographically in either a common law jurisdiction with an elective share statute or a community property jurisdiction. Keep in mind that you must consider the possibility that the couple may move to another state during their marriage. Your professor may specify that the laws of a specific jurisdiction will apply to this exercise. If the professor does not specify the applicable law, the following statutes should be used. With respect to enforceability of the agreement, assume that the Uniform Premarital Agreement Act applies. With respect to legal protections for a surviving spouse at the death of a married person, if you are in a common law state, assume that the Uniform Probate Code and its intestacy and elective share provisions (section 2-102 and sections 2-201 through 2-214) apply. If you are in a community property state, assume that the provisions of the Uniform Marital Property Act apply with respect to protections at the death of a spouse. For principles of property division and maintenance at dissolution, if you are in a common law state, assume that the Uniform Marriage and Divorce Act applies. If you are in a community property state, assume again that the UMPA applies for property division and maintenance at divorce. Links to these statutes are on the website.

TASK 1: Review the form prenuptial agreement on the website. Note that the agreement requires that the lawyers provide a written memorandum to the clients explaining the rights that they would otherwise have in each other's property at death and at divorce. Prepare this memorandum summarizing the rights of married persons in their spouse's property under the applicable state law. Remember that the memo is to be read by your layperson clients, so it must be written in language that they can understand.

TASK 2: In this task, students negotiate the terms of a prenuptial agreement for the couple and prepare the agreement. If done with four students, each student playing the client will review the confidential client file on the website for his or her role only. The students playing the lawyers will not review the client files but will interview their own clients for the information.

If done with two students, each student will assume the role of lawyer for one of the parties and will review only the confidential client file for his or her client.

Once facts are gathered, the two lawyers (and the clients, if four students involved), will negotiate the terms of the agreement. The form prenuptial agreement on the website will be used as a basis for drafting the final agreement.

Negotiation can be done at a meeting of all parties, or done with the attorneys alone who then discuss the proposals with their clients.

RESOURCES

Additional resources are available on the LexisNexis Web Course that was created for this book.

Andersen, *Understanding Trusts and Estates* Chapter 8 (4th ed.)

**DO NOT PROCEED TO NEXT PAGE UNTIL YOU HAVE
COMPLETED EXERCISE**

SELF STUDY

<u>TASK 1:</u> There is a sample memorandum for a common law state and a sample memorandum for a community property state on the website.

<u>TASK 2:</u>

Each negotiation should produce a unique document based on the issues that the parties playing the clients decided to emphasize. A sample prenuptial agreement drafted using the facts in the problem is on the website, but there is no one "correct" document.

In negotiating and drafting, you should have considered the following issues:

1. <u>Ethics</u>

   a. Was it ethical for Mia's parents' lawyer to represent her in the negotiation? If you were that lawyer, did you think about achieving their goals or Mia's goals? If there was a conflict between the two, did you try to steer her towards her parents' intentions? See RPC 1.7.

   b. If you were Howard's lawyer, what ethical issues were raised by Mia's parents paying your bill? Would that fact affect how strenuously you advocate for Howard? See RPC 1.8.

   c. If you were Howard's lawyer, were you more concerned with ensuring that your client received as much financial protection as the other side would give or with following Howard's desire not to make trouble? See RPC 1.4. One of the most difficult challenges for a lawyer is balancing the client's desires with what the lawyer thinks is best for the client. See also RPC 1.14. This problem is particularly difficult when representing a client in negotiating a prenuptial agreement, because the client often is unable to view his or her future spouse as an adversary, may not want the prenuptial agreement at all and may assume that the agreement is unnecessary because they will never get divorced. This can be risky for the lawyer; the lawyer may be sued for malpractice if he or she allows the client to sign a prenuptial agreement that leaves the client too vulnerable, even if at the time the client wants to sign it.

2. <u>Making the agreement enforceable</u>

   a. Section 6 of the UPAA specifies what is necessary to make a prenuptial agreement enforceable. The first requirement is that the agreement is entered into voluntarily by the parties.

How did you insure that the agreement was voluntary? Critical factors include timing (was the agreement negotiated and signed well in advance of the wedding, or was the requirement of a prenuptial agreement brought up just a week before the wedding), whether either party gave an ultimatum and when, and whether each party was represented by counsel. The UPAA does not require each party to have counsel but representation is one indication that the agreement was entered into voluntarily.

b. The UPAA further provides that an agreement that is unconscionable is not enforceable, unless other requirements are met. How much consideration was given to providing some support to the poorer party (Howard), so that the agreement would not be considered unconscionable under the UPAA? See Restatement (Third) of Property: Wills and Other Donative Transfers section 9.4 (2003). The UPAA does not define unconscionability, but according to the comments it borrowed the notion from the Uniform Marriage and Divorce Act. That Act's comments include overreaching, concealment of assets and aggressive negotiation inconsistent with the obligations of marital partners to deal fairly with each other as indications of unconscionability. The disparity in Mia and Howard's financial circumstances is one indication of unconscionability that must be overcome. Another factor indicating unconscionability is an unrepresented party, but that is not a factor under this fact pattern. Unconscionability is also determined by comparing the terms of the agreement with what the parties would be entitled to in the absence of an agreement. Could the terms of your agreement viewed as a whole be unconscionable? Specific terms of your agreement as compared to legal protections waived is discussed below.

c. Was there full disclosure of the parties' assets and liabilities? How did you handle disclosure of Mia's trust and her anticipated inheritance? The UPAA provides that an agreement is not enforceable if it is unconscionable and the agreement does not pass the financial disclosure test. In order to pass this test, each party must have made fair and reasonable disclosure of assets, the challenging party made an express, voluntary waiver of full disclosure, or the challenging party knew or should have known the extent and nature of the other party's assets. Did you include in the agreement a waiver of disclosure that would have satisfied the Act's requirements?

    d.   Did each lawyer fully disclose to the parties what they would be entitled to without a prenuptial agreement, so that each party would know what they were gaining or giving up by signing the agreement? How did you ensure that your client fully understood the terms of the agreement?

3.   Provisions at Death of One Spouse

    a.   How did your provisions take into account what each party would have been entitled to under state law (either elective share statutes or community property regime)?

    b.   Did you include a complete waiver of rights on death of first spouse? If yes, did you rely on the spouses to sign Wills after marriage or did you include provisions requiring certain provisions for the survivor at the death of one spouse? Often the assumption is that required provisions for the surviving spouse at death are not necessary because, unlike divorce, the spouses want to take care of each other at death and will prepare Wills to take care of each other. However, often the spouses do not get around to the necessary estate planning or the estate plan is not effective for some reason. Mandatory provisions for the poorer spouse at death in the prenuptial agreement are necessary if there is a waiver of legal protections at death (such as elective share and homestead provisions), because if for some reason there is no effective estate planning the surviving spouse can file a claim in the estate to enforce the provisions in the prenuptial agreement.

4.   Provisions for Divorce

    a.   Did you protect Mia's celebrity status and career goodwill? See *Piscopo v. Piscopo*, 557 A.2d 1040 (1989).

    b.   Did you protect Harold with maintenance if he becomes a stay at home dad and gives up the shoe shop?

    c.   Did you key property awards to Harold based on the length of the marriage, similar to the UPC elective share provisions?

    d.   How did you deal with Mia's lack of liquidity (she currently spends all salary and her remaining assets are tied up in the trust; her parents are likely to put her inheritance in trust as well)?

Chapter 10

TRUSTS: DISCRETIONARY TRUSTS

INTRODUCTION

Settlors (and testators) have enormous flexibility — limited at the extremes by public policy — to craft trusts that will meet the individual needs of their families. The challenge for lawyers is to create (and encourage their clients to create) the best available solutions. Effective communication is the key to achieving that goal.

Lawyers, especially as they become more experienced, are tempted to pigeonhole clients: "Client J's situation reminds me of what we did for Client C a few years ago, so let's do that here." A better approach would offer a range of options designed to stimulate thinking and encourage Client J to come up with new ones. Then, Client J might choose an entirely different approach, one better suited to J's family. Remember: in this context, when a client asks "Could I do this:......?", the answer is almost always, "Yes." The key to success is getting the client thinking, for the client knows the nuances of the family setting much better than the lawyer ever can.

This exercise presents you with a family that, like all families, has individuals with different needs and temperaments. You don't have the advantage of holding the kind of discussions contemplated above, so you'll have to assume they have taken place. Those conversations should have covered questions like these:

- Preserving flexibility over time requires giving discretion somewhere. Should it all be with the trustee or should others be involved? Who should have the final say (and responsibility)?

- Are you concerned that the trustee will be too stingy? Or not frugal enough?

- Are there words that can capture the sense of how much discretion the decisionmakers should have? Meeting "necessary" expenses? Providing support "appropriate for the circumstances"? Some other standard?

- What sorts of benefits should the trust offer? General support? Health care? Housing? Vacations? New business ventures?

Education? If so, for what sorts of schools, covering which costs, subject to what restrictions?

- For ease of administration, the trustee probably should have the authority to provide funds either to the beneficiaries or directly to others. Who should be those "others"? Caregivers? Dependents? Others in the household? Suppliers of services? Landlords?

- Should you name a trust advisor or advocate for any of the beneficiaries, either from the start or if the person should become disabled? By what definition or means should we identify someone as "disabled"? What would be the trust advisor/advocate's relationship to the trustee? Advise the trustee? Direct the trustee?

- Crucial medical information might be protected by the Health Insurance Portability and Accountability Act [HIPAA], 42 U.S.C. § 1320(d). Should the trust authorize someone to access that information? Who?

- Should some of the beneficiaries (which?) have the authority to withdraw trust assets (how much? how often?) without the trustee's permission? Only if they get a trust advisor's *permission*? Only after *consulting* with the trustee or trust advisor?

As you develop the draft(s) this exercise requires, assume that you and the client have resolved questions like those (and others that those questions prompt in your mind). Structure your draft(s) to reflect the approaches your client chose.

Especially with more complex documents, lawyers may not create a first draft for the entire project at one time. Even if some issues are still unresolved, it may make sense to create part of the draft while ideas are still fresh in the mind. When working on just a portion of a document, visualize the whole thing. Where in the document do you see this language appearing? It will be easier to put everything together later if along the way you have created appropriate headings and sub-headings as you develop each section. For other suggestions, see the introductory sections to chapters 2, 3, & 5 of this book.

Another drafting hint, especially for complex documents: schedule down time. Let your draft get "cold" before you review it. That way, it's easier to see it as others will.

SKILLS INVOLVED: Developing and evaluating strategies. Drafting.

GENERAL DESCRIPTION OF EXERCISE: Draft language defining the scope of a trustee's discretionary power over income and principal to benefit three siblings with different ages, temperaments, abilities, and needs.

PARTICIPANTS NEEDED: This exercise can be done solo or in teams.

ESTIMATED TIME REQUIRED:

Task 1: 30–60 minutes.

Task 2: 30–60 minutes.

Task 3: 30–60 minutes.

LEVEL OF DIFFICULTY (1–5):

ROLE IN EXERCISE: You represent a single parent with adult children. You will (1) develop planning strategies that anticipate the children's different needs and (2) draft trust language to reflect those strategies.

THE EXERCISE

You are to draft portions of a trust agreement for Rosa Pineda. Divorced when her children were young, she is the mother of three adults: Emilia (29), Jaime (27), and Carlota (23). As a single mother working as a bookkeeper, Rosa struggled to support her family. Five years ago, she inherited from her father enough assets to allow her to live comfortably, but frugally, while working part-time. She's tired of obsessing about investments and wants to establish a lifetime trust, with a local bank as trustee. She'll reserve a right to claim whatever amounts of income and principal she desires during her lifetime. At her death, the funds will go to her children (or grandchildren).

Rosa has decided that, if all children survive her and are under age 40, the trustee will create three equal shares, one for each child. In each case, Rosa will give the trustee the power to use trust assets for her children, according to the standards articulated in the trust. The trust for each will continue for 17 years after Rosa's death, or until the beneficiary reaches age 40 (or dies), whichever comes first. At that point, the share will go to the child (or to various survivors).

Your part of the project is to draft standards defining the limits of the trustee's discretion to expend trust assets for Rosa's children. Rosa is concerned because of the different ways her children responded to $10,000 gifts each received when their grandfather died. Here is that family history.

1. Emilia Pineda, a college graduate who runs her own moderately-successful advertising business, is married to Antonio Gialatti (23). They have one child (3) and are hoping for at least one more. Antonio is a musician who works irregularly in regional venues, but does manage to bring in some extra spending money from time to time. After soul-searching about whether to expand her business, Emilia decided to use her $10,000 inheritance as seed money for a tour for Antonio. Antonio, who is easily tempted to live beyond his means, finished the tour with empty coffers.

    Rosa believes Emilia is level-headed and good with money. At different times, Rosa has lent Emilia money to help her business grow, and Emilia has always repaid on time. Rosa's first instinct was simply to give Emilia one-third of the assets after Rosa's death. However, Rosa is not too fond of Antonio. He's kind to his wife and daughter, but he seems lazy and self-indulgent. Rosa fears that if Emilia inherited an outright gift, she might again succumb to the temptation to try to "support Antonio's dream," rather than investing in her business or saving for her children's college educations.

2. Jaime Pineda is unmarried and living in a halfway house. Since his late teens, he's been in and out of trouble (including a stint at a juvenile facility that made enough of an impression that he's never been to jail as an adult). The main cause: addiction to alcohol, with an attraction for "recreational drugs" along the way. Unsurprisingly, Jaime used the inheritance from his grandfather to support his habits. However, he has been sober for almost a year, earned his G.E.D, and has a full-time job loading trucks for a shipping firm. It looks like he's finally

gotten it together, but Rosa worries how long this will last, and what she can do to help the process.

3.　Carlota Santos is married to Marco Santos (23). They have no children. Like her brother, Carlota was a rebellious teen. At 17, she ran away and lived on the streets for three months before Rosa located her and forcibly took her to a detox facility, where she discovered she has some skill at painting landscapes. Since that time, Carlota has been off drugs. When her grandfather died, Carlota was attending a community college to become a certified X-ray technician. She used half of his gift for a spring break trip to Mexico and half toward tuition. She's now working at a local hospital. Last year, she and Marco were married. He's an accountant for a Fortune 500 company.

Carlota is in some ways like her brother-in-law, Antonio. She'd like to live better than she can afford to. Between them, Marco and Carlota have a steady income that Rosa thinks should be enough for them to be saving to buy a house and putting something away for emergencies. Instead, they seem to live hand-to-mouth. Rosa hears about new clothes and weekends at expensive resorts, but also gets requests for short term loans (always repaid) to get them over a "crunch." Rosa is searching for a mechanism to encourage Carlota to be more financially responsible.

Do **NOT** draft the language necessary to divide the trust after Rosa's death or to establish alternative beneficiaries of the children's shares. Limit your draft to articulating standards for using the trust assets.

You may want to create definitions to help flesh-out requirements while avoiding long, tangled sentences. If you use definitions, put them in a separate section. A standard approach is to identify the buzz word by punctuation or a different format, followed by "means" or "includes." (e.g. "Education" means....)

TASK 1: Create standards for using the trust assets on behalf of Emilia Pineda.

TASK 2: Create standards for using the trust assets on behalf of Jaime Pineda.

TASK 3: Create standards for using the trust assets on behalf of Carlota Santos.

REFERENCES

Additional resources are available on the LexisNexis Web Course that was created for this book.

Roger W. Andersen, *Understanding Trusts & Estates* §§ 13 & 31 (4th ed. 2009)

Roger W. Andersen, *Plan While You Can: Legal Solutions for Facing Disability (2003)* pgs. 53–62

DO NOT PROCEED TO THE NEXT PAGE UNTIL YOU HAVE COMPLETED THE EXERCISE

SELF-STUDY

- Are there still too many words?

- Imagine yourself a trustee looking for guidance. If you were facing a multi-page document, could you easily find the relevant section? Do the headings clearly indicate the content?

- Imagine yourself a trustee looking for guidance. Does the document help you decide whether you could (should) spend trust assets if:

    1. Emilia and Marco want to put a family room on their house.

    2. Jaime is injured at work, needs a wheelchair, and needs housing that can accommodate one, for 3 months.

    3. Jaime suffers a relapse and needs 2 months in a dry-out facility.

    4. Carlota, contemplating having children and nervous about exposure on the job, has decided to pursue an art career. She's asking for funds to spend 6 months in Italy, touring museums and taking lessons. Marco is seeking a short-term transfer to Rome, but if that doesn't work out, he would take a leave of absence to accompany her. Then they'd need to cover joint living expenses, or live apart.

- Rosa is concerned about Marco's work ethic. Maybe she also doubts whether the marriage will last. Should the trustee's discretion to spend for Emilia be liberalized if Marco is no longer in the picture? Would such a provision violate public policy for encouraging divorce?

- Consider whether the same person could serve as trust advisor for different beneficiaries or should have the same authority/ duties for each.

- Think of siblings you know and consider whether you would treat them differently if you were their parent creating an estate plan.

SAMPLE DRAFT

Excerpts from Rosa Pineda's trust are available on the LEXISNEXIS online platform.

Chapter 11

TRUSTS: CHARITABLE

INTRODUCTION

By creating tax incentives and by exempting charitable trusts from the Rule Against Perpetuities, the law encourages individuals to support organizations that are beneficial to the community. As times change, however, it may become impossible or impractical to continue to pursue a particular charitable purpose. Lawyers who help create charitable institutions or who draft documents giving property to those institutions should preserve flexibility to meet such new circumstances. One approach is to cast a broad net in the first place by allowing a variety of possible uses. Another (not inconsistent with the first) is to provide alternative takers or uses if the first choice doesn't work out.

When trust documents are not flexible, petitions become necessary, asking courts to apply the cy pres doctrine to modify or terminate the trust. Caution: several states circumscribe their courts' cy pres power more narrowly than does Uniform Trust Code § 413. In particular, the UTC establishes a presumption that the trust settlor met the cy pres doctrine's requirement of a general charitable intent (as opposed to an intention just to benefit specific goals or charities).

This chapter affords the opportunity to view the problem from both sides. You are asked first to develop strategies for preserving flexibility. Then you are asked to prepare a cy pres petition because a document was inadequately drafted in the first place.

SKILLS INVOLVED: Strategic planning; statutory interpretation; drafting a petition.

GENERAL DESCRIPTION OF EXERCISE: Developing strategies to avoid the need for applying the cy pres doctrine to a charitable trust and preparing a cy pres petition for an inadequately-drafted trust.

PARTICIPANTS NEEDED: One student.

ESTIMATED TIME REQUIRED:

Task 1: 15–30 minutes

Task 2: 30–45 minutes

LEVEL OF DIFFICULTY (1–5):

ROLE IN EXERCISE: Task 1: You represent a client seeking to establish a charitable trust.

Task 2: You represent a trustee charged with administering a charitable trust.

APPLICABLE LAW: Unless directed otherwise, assume your jurisdiction has adopted Uniform Trust Code § 413.

THE EXERCISE

TASK 1:

You practice law in Centerville, a thriving county seat, about 30 miles from Dusty, a small farming town that keeps getting smaller. Next week, you will be meeting with a longtime client, Winston Willingham III, an affluent widower in his early 60's, whose parents are deceased and who has no children. He'd like to do what he can to support the town and help it grow. He's told you that after his death, he wishes his substantial fortune to be used, for as long as the law permits, to provide Winston Willingham Memorial Scholarships to graduates of Dusty High School so they can continue their educations. You anticipate the possibility that Dusty's population may shrink so much that the school will close and Dusty students will attend a consolidated school elsewhere. In preparation for your meeting with Willingham, prepare a memo to the file identifying areas where you need more information and outlining approaches he might take to both benefit Dusty students and foster education if the school closes.

TASK 2:

Assume you moved to Centerville five years after Winston Willingham III died. You represent Centerville National Bank, trustee of the Winston Willingham Memorial Scholarship Trust. As you might guess, Dusty High School closed this past summer, and students from Dusty now attend Benton County High School. The key language in Willingham's trust reads as follows:

> The Trustee shall, to the maximum extent possible, use the income from this trust to offset the costs of undergraduate, post-secondary education for graduates of Dusty High School at schools of their choice. Such costs include tuition, books and supplies, room and board, and expenses incurred to travel home.

The bank would like to continue to operate the trust and has asked you to prepare a cy pres petition to be presented to the local judge of general jurisdiction in the county. Prepare the petition.

REFERENCES

Additional resources are available on the LexisNexis Web Course that was created for this book.

Roger W. Andersen, *Understanding Trusts & Estates* (4th ed. 2009)

Uniform Trust Code § 413

DO NOT PROCEED TO THE NEXT PAGE UNTIL YOU HAVE COMPLETED THE EXERCISE

SELF-STUDY

- How well did you anticipate the kinds questions that could come up when administering the trust? Does "education" include ballet lessons? Mechanic's training? Trips abroad? Public? Private? Who picks the school/program? Any minimum grade point? Maximum time? Can a child drop out and return? For any reason or only for a "good" reason (e.g., illness or military service)?

  What expenses are covered? Tuition only? Room (who picks it?)? Board (how fancy? What about beer money?)? Travel home (elsewhere?)? Books? Fees? A new computer? Passports?

  Notice that the more detail, the less flexibility. Willingham may have strong feelings on some issues and not care about others; the document you ultimately draft should reflect those difference.

- Willingham really cares about Dusty as a town and hopes it will survive. Should the scholarships be dependent on a promise to return to the Dusty area after graduation for, say, three years? Is that feasible, in light of limited employment opportunities? Would it unfairly benefit farmers, as opposed to "townies"? Would it help if the fund covered costs incurred during a period (how long?) of transition to full-time work/career?

- If Willingham is afraid the school will close, should the purpose be expanded to include financial support for the high school?

- Did you consider broadening the class of beneficiaries to include all students in, say, the county? But wouldn't that undercut Willingham's effort to help the town of Dusty to survive? Should the first choice be Dusty H.S. students, with others eligible only if the school closes?

SAMPLE DRAFTS

Additional resources, including sample draft documents, are available on the LexisNexis Web Course that was created for this book.

Chapter 12

TRUSTS: CREATING FUTURE INTERESTS

INTRODUCTION

In the modern world, estate planners use the "system of estates" to create interests in trusts. The primary building blocks are life estates (usually for the settlor's generation, but sometimes also for the next one) and contingent remainders (usually contingent on survival of a life tenant or to a specific age).

While "standard" patterns have emerged (see, e.g., Chapter 2), drafters face the continuing challenge of creating language that fits both the structure and the needs of each client's family. Perhaps the most common drafting mistake is to assume that younger beneficiaries will survive older ones. Good drafting anticipates the possibility that beneficiaries could "die in the wrong order." It creates alternative gifts to deal with that situation.

Developing a clearly-structured, clearly-labeled organizational scheme is the key to producing a draft trust document than can handle the complexity of a series of both successive and alternative gifts. The drafting gets much easier if you know where you're going. One approach is to create a decision tree. An example is available on the Skills and Values website. That gives you a visual check of whether you've established an appropriate organization and hierarchy. Are like things grouped together? Have you articulated a heading that covers related sub-topics? You also can use the outline as a checklist to see if you've dealt with all the issues. (e.g., In each situation that you require survival, also specify what happens if the person does not survive.) Once you have the skeleton, then add the details.

When filling in those details, recall the "divide into as many shares as [you need at that time]" approach identified in Chapter 2. For ideas on how to use the device in the context of creating future interests (rather than just in a will giving shares as of the testator's death), see UPC § 2-709(b) & (c). By the way, using the terminology "then-surviving" (rather than merely "surviving") leaves less room for confusion.

Clients who have few close relatives or who establish trusts that can last a long time may run out of possible beneficiaries who they can identify by name or close relationship. At that point there may be a tendency for clients to say (or lawyers to suggest), "Just give it to the heirs." Of course, that's a perfectly legitimate response, but that's also a good time to consider whether the client would prefer to make a charitable gift. After all, by the time they get down to "heirs," they're not thinking about people by name. Clients might not even know who those folks would be. Sometimes, a charity might be closer than a relative. It's worth asking.

Trusts giving property to someone's "heirs" should answer questions about how, exactly, to identify those heirs. Timing is particularly important. You'll recall that we typically determine who a person's heirs are as of that person's death. That approach creates real problems if, for example, the heirs take a remainder following a life estate. Between the time of the settlor's death (when the heirs are identified and their remainders vest) and the end of the life estate, some of those heirs may have died. When the life tenant dies, we may have to re-open the estates of the now-deceased heirs to see who gets the trust property. A better solution is for the trust to direct that the "heirs" be identified as if the settlor had died when the disposition is to take effect in possession or enjoyment. In our example, that would mean as of the death of the life tenant. Recall the principle: give property to warm bodies.

Gifts to "heirs" also raise the question of which statute to apply. To avoid having to dig back to see what the law was at a particular time, the best solution is to apply the law of the decedent's domicile in effect when you are determining who the heirs are. For statutory language you can adapt, see UPC § 2-711.

Finally, gifts to heirs raise the risk that a court might apply the Doctrine of Worthier Title to invalidate the gift. In the states that still follow the doctrine, you can overcome it with clear language in the will. To be safe, you should say that not only the doctrine should not apply to your document, but also reiterate that the settlor intends to create a remainder interest in his or her heirs.

SKILLS INVOLVED: Drafting.

GENERAL DESCRIPTION OF EXERCISE: Draft language that creates both present and future interests among a client's family.

PARTICIPANTS NEEDED: This can be a solo or a small-group exercise.

ESTIMATED TIME REQUIRED:

Task 1(A): 2–3 hours

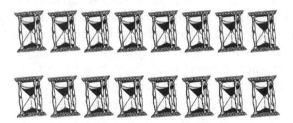

Task 1(B): 4–5 hours

Task 2: 30 minutes

LEVEL OF DIFFICULTY (1–5):

ROLE IN EXERCISE: You have the choice of representing (1) a late-middle aged couple with adult children or (2) a younger couple with young children. In either case, you will be drafting language for a trust that will benefit both generations.

THE EXERCISE

TASK 1: Select one of the following projects:

A)   Juan and Karen Hidalgo are in their 50's and have two adult children, one of whom is married. They have no grandchildren.

To avoid probate, they want to establish a lifetime trust in which they will act as joint trustees during their lifetimes. During that time, the trustee will pay them whatever amounts of income and principal as they direct. After one dies, the other will continue as sole trustee, acting under the same arrangement. After the death of the survivor, the trust will end and the assets be distributed to Juan and Karen's descendants, according to a per capita at each generation scheme. If no descendants survive, the assets go to a charity [you choose].

Draft **ONLY** the language necessary to create the various interests of Juan, Karen, their descendants, and the charity. Do not draft other language necessary to create the trust itself or govern its administration. Assume terms like "children" and "survive" are defined elsewhere in the document. Depending upon the structure you adopt, you may need to define "per capita at each generation." Once you have finished the draft, put it down for a day or two and then recheck it — looking especially for gaps in the disposition and for ways to cut additional language — before moving on to the self-study section.

B) Juan and Karen Hidalgo are in their mid-30's. They want to establish a trust for their three young daughters (and any later children) who may be under age 25 when both Juan and Karen have died. For now, they will use an unfunded revocable living trust that will simply serve as a possible receptacle of their life insurance and of the residue of their probate estates. However, they may later want to add funds to the trust during their lifetimes. (For example, they may inherit assets and need management, or one may become disabled and need support after the other's death.) To preserve the option of using the trust during both Juan and Karen's lifetimes, the trust should give them the right to receive "such amounts of income and principal as the Trustee determines appropriate for their support.".

After the survivor's death, Juan and Karen's descendants will share the trust on a strict per stirpes basis, but with the twist that some shares could remain in trust. Three categories of descendants will share: (1) the children 25 or older will get their shares outright, (2) shares of children under 25 will be held in trust, and (3) shares of children who have died but who leave descendants surviving Juan and Karen's survivor will go directly to those descendants. [This is not a good plan — there should be a further trust for minors — but it keeps this exercise manageable.]

If the trust continues for children under 25, each of those children will get "such amounts of income and principal as the Trustee determines appropriate for their support" until age 25, with the balance of each share distributed as each child reaches 25. If the child dies before reaching 25, distribute that child's share first to the child's children. If there are none, distribute the child's share as appropriate to (1) the siblings then over 25, (2) the on-going trusts for siblings under 25, or (3) the then-surviving children of non-surviving siblings. [Again, on-going trusts for minors would be a better plan, but ignore that for the purpose of this exercise.] Finally, there should be an ultimate remainder [in case of no siblings or their children at any time after the death of Juan and Karen's survivor] to a charity you identify.

Draft **ONLY** the language necessary to create the various interests of Juan, Karen, their descendants, and the charity. Do not draft other language necessary to create the trust itself or govern its administration. Assume terms like "children" and "survive" are defined elsewhere in the document. Once you have finished the draft, put it down for a day or two and then recheck it — looking especially for ways to cut additional language and for gaps in the disposition — before moving on to the self-assessment section.

TASK 2— Instead of giving the ultimate remainder to charity, draft a new clause giving the trust property to Juan's heirs; assume your jurisdiction recognizes the Doctrine of Worthier Title.

REFERENCES

Additional resources are available on the LexisNexis Web Course that was created for this book.

Uniform Probate Code § 2-711

Roger W. Andersen, *Understanding Trusts & Estates* §§ 34[C], 35[B][2][b], 44[D][1] & [3] (4th ed. 2009)

DO NOT PROCEED TO THE NEXT PAGE UNTIL YOU HAVE COMPLETED THE EXERCISE

SELF-STUDY

- Examine your organization. Do the topics follow in a logical order? Usually chronological order works best. Are there visual clues for which topics are sub-topics of another? For example, if you have a series of alternative gifts that might take place at a certain time (like the death of a life tenant), is each alternative identified separately? Tabulation often helps clarify substance.

- Consider your use of headings. Can you easily find which sections apply to a particular beneficiary?

- Can you eliminate words? Can you find "in the event that" or "on the condition that"? Both mean "if."

- Review the way you handled survivorship requirements.

  1. Is it clear *who* the beneficiary had to survive?

  2. Is there *always* an alternative beneficiary provided, in case the primary beneficiary has not survived?

  3. Have you paired "survive" and "predecease" in the same setting? The project assumes you have a definition of "survive" that includes a time period. Unless you also assume that "predecease" has been defined to take the same time into account, pairing those terms can leave a gap. For example, if the time period is 5 days, and the beneficiary lives for only 2, the beneficiary has not "survived" according to the definition, but also has not predeceased.

  4. For Task 1 (B), suppose one of Juan & Karen's children survives both of them, but then dies before reaching age 25. Does your draft cover what to do with that person's share?

- Have you employed the "divide into as many shares as...." technique without creating more shares than you need (and then having to dispose of those)? For example, suppose Juan & Karen's son dies before they do and leaves no descendants. Would your draft create two shares or only one (the correct method) after the death of Juan & Karen's survivor?

- Did you use the tabulation technique when you identified the various categories into which the trust would be divided after the death of the surviving settlor?

- When applying a condition to a group, have you said, for example, "my children who survive me," instead of the ambiguous "my children if they survive me"? To see the difference, suppose two of three children survived. Would anyone take under the second formulation?

- Does your document assume that only Juan or Karen will be Trustee? It should be phrased broadly enough to anticipate the need for a third-party successor trustee after the death, disability or resignation of Juan and Karen's survivor.

- Does the gift to Juan's heirs clearly identify what statute applies? Does it only give property to people who are then alive? Does it avoid application of the Doctrine of Worthier Title?

SAMPLE DRAFT

Additional resources, including sample draft documents, are available on the LexisNexis Web Course that was created for this book.

Chapter 13

TRUSTS: POWERS OF APPOINTMENT

INTRODUCTION

Powers of appointment are the lifeblood of trusts' adaptability over time. A power of appointment is a power one person has to designate who will take property subject to the power or what shares the takers will receive. For example, a settlor might create a trust giving a life estate to the settlor's spouse and also giving the spouse a power of appointment to designate how the remainder after that life estate will be distributed. That way, a client can establish the essential features of an estate plan, but postpone many decisions until closer to the time the property actually will be divided. Because they preserve the option of responding to unanticipated events, powers of appointment are among the most useful of the tools available to estate planners.

First, a brief reminder on terminology. The **donor** is the person who creates the power. The person who gets the power is called the **donee**. Note that in this context we're talking about who gets *the right to exercise the power*, not necessarily who ultimately gets to enjoy or spend the property subject to the power. The donee can give the property only to people the donor identifies as **objects** (aka "**permissible appointees**") of the power, which may or may not include the donee. If the donee exercises the power, the recipient is called an **appointee**. To the extent the donee does not exercise the power, the property goes to a **taker in default of appointment**, if the donor so provided. The same person may assume several roles.

Lawyers see powers at both ends. Sometimes lawyers design and draft new powers of appointment as one piece of an estate plan. Sometimes they draft documents exercising powers that have been created earlier. This chapter offers the opportunity to work with powers of appointment in both contexts.

Designing a power of appointment requires considering both the needs of the current client and the problems that could arise if the power is later exercised. At the outset, tax considerations often predominate. Subject to some refinements, if the donee of a power can give the property subject to the power to herself, her creditors, her estate or its creditors, then the power is called a "general power" and the property is included in the donee's gross estate for federal tax purposes. Depending upon the tax plan (beyond the scope of this exercise), someone might want or not want that consequence. Because property subject to a general power is one step away from the donee's absolute ownership, general powers offer the ultimate in flexibility.

A great deal of flexibility can be achieved, however, while at the same time keeping the property out of the donee's gross estate. Powers that allow property to be appointed to anyone other than the big four (self, creditors, estate, estate's creditors) are often called "hybrid" powers and do not bring the property into the donee's gross estate. More narrowly, many clients opt to create "special" powers that can only be exercised in favor of a class of objects (like "children") that does not include the donee. This approach allows donors to maintain some control over an estate plan, but preserve flexibility. Recall the example in the first paragraph of this section.

You may see references to "non-general" powers, grouping special and hybrid powers because neither brings property into a gross estate. Lawyers and courts still commonly refer to "general" and "special" powers, and you should understand the terms according to their context. In most situations, "general" probably means a power exercisable in favor of the donee, his estate, his creditors, or its creditors. If the question involves tax, "special" probably means "not general." If the question does not involve tax, "special" means "for a limited class of objects" that excludes the donee, the donee's creditors, the donee's estate or creditors of the donee's estate as class members.

You can see that lawyers creating powers must pay special attention to the breadth of the class of objects. Both different tax consequences and different levels of discretion in the hands of the donee flow from that element.

Another concern is the mechanics of how the power can be exercised later. Donors can create powers exercisable by a document during the donee's lifetime (inter-vivos powers), exercisable by a will at death (testamentary powers), or exercisable either way at the donee's option.

Donors also can give specific instructions for donees to follow in order to exercise their powers. Two devices are especially useful. Donors can prevent questions about whether the donee actually intended to exercise the power by requiring the donee to refer specifically to the power being exercised. By postponing the time in which a power can be exercised until after the donor's death or incapacity, the donor can insure that the donee is at least acting on information that is not available to the donor.

Drafters of special powers should be alert to a particular set of potential problems. Because special powers limit donees' choices of appointees, some courts have viewed special powers as somehow smaller than general powers in other respects as well. This limited view of the authority granted by special powers is losing favor, but, because of the risk that a court may take a narrow view, good drafting requires donors of special powers to be particularly careful to identify the sorts of interests they want their donees to be able to create. Special powers also present the question of how much discretion the donee has to choose among the class of objects. When the goal is to preserve the maximum amount of flexibility, a donee should have an "exclusionary" power, one that allows leaving out some of the permissible appointees when it comes time to exercise the power.

In many situations, clients expect that the powers they create will *not* ever be exercised. The powers may be there to achieve a tax result or preserve flexibility to respond to something unusual, but unless something special happens, the basic plan of disposition will continue unaffected. Effectively, language identifying "takers in default" points to the heart of the dispository scheme. Think of gift-in-default language as parallel to a residuary clause: say that it applies "to the extent that" (rather than "if") the power is not exercised. That way, if the power is exercised, but not completely, the default instructions still apply. Because the default instructions are often the primary plan, they can get complex. Rather than adding to the complexity by folding them in with the language creating the power of appointment, many drafters prefer to use a cross-reference. The takers-in-default clause says that if it applies, the trust property shall be held and distributed "according to the terms of Article ...."

The primary principle for exercising powers of appointment sounds simple: follow the rules. Find and carefully read the document that created the power. What documents are required? What objects are within the scope of the power? What interests can be created when exercising the power?

The rest of exercising a power of appointment is substantially the same as making any other disposition. After all, that's what a power of appointment does: it disposes of one person's property according to directions given by another. Of course, drafting any disposition can be a tricky business in its own right.

SKILLS INVOLVED: Drafting

GENERAL DESCRIPTION OF EXERCISE: Draft language to create and to exercise powers of appointment.

PARTICIPANTS NEEDED: This can be a solo or a small-group exercise.

ESTIMATED TIME REQUIRED:

Task 1: 60–75 minutes

Task 2: 45–60 minutes

LEVEL OF DIFFICULTY (1–5):

ROLE IN EXERCISE: This project gives you the opportunity to view powers of appointment from two perspectives. First, you'll represent one client (the donor of the power) who wants create a special, testamentary power for his daughter (the donee of the power). Second, we'll imagine time has passed and you are representing the donee of that power, who now wants appropriate language in her will to exercise the power. We look at both ends of the process, because lawyers whose language creates powers must have in mind how they will be exercised, and lawyers whose language exercises powers must be sure to follow the rules established at the time those powers were created.

THE EXERCISE

TASK 1:

Your client, Henry Harrison, is creating a lifetime trust. He's retaining a life estate for himself and also creating second life estate to benefit his daughter, Maryanne Harrison. Because Henry expects Maryanne to survive him by many years, Henry also wants to give Maryanne a special, testamentary power of appointment to allocate the trust property among Henry's descendants who survive Maryanne. Draft **ONLY** the trust section that would create Maryanne's power. Use a separate section, so it will be easy for others to find the relevant language when reviewing the document. Imagine that it appears directly after the section that describes Maryanne's life interest. Provide that a gift in default would go "as follows:...." and leave the rest blank.

TASK 2:

Assume Henry has died and that you now represent Maryanne, who needs a new will and wants to exercise the power she got from her father. Maryanne wants the property to go to her children. Make up names, dates, shares, and alternative gifts you'd like to create. Draft **ONLY** the language necessary for Maryanne to exercise the power (not the whole will).

REFERENCES

Roger W. Andersen, *Understanding Trusts & Estates* ch. 10 (4th ed. 2009)

DO NOT PROCEED TO THE NEXT PAGE UNTIL YOU HAVE COMPLETED THE EXERCISE

SELF-STUDY

Review your draft of Henry's trust section to see how clearly it answers the following questions:

- What happens to the trust property after Maryanne's death (i.e., at the time the power goes into operation)?

- How, exactly, can Maryanne go about exercising the power?

- Must she wait until after Henry's death to execute the documents necessary to exercise the power?

- Can Maryanne use the power to direct that the property from Henry's trust go to a new trust? If so, can she create new powers of appointment that would apply to the property in the new trust?

- Can she create different size shares for different permissible appointees? Can she leave some out?

- WHAT HAPPENS IF MARYANNE DOESN'T EXERCISE HER POWER?

- What happens if she only partially exercises the power? For example, assume she creates a life estate, but creates a gap by saying nothing more. If you said the gift-in-default applies "*if* Maryanne fails to effectively exercise her power of appointment." [emphasis added], you left open the argument that the default clause doesn't apply because Maryanne has exercised the power (just not completely). You got it right if you said the gift-in-default applies "*to the extent that* Maryanne fails to effectively exercise her power of appointment." [emphasis added] That language lets the default clause operate much like a residuary clause in a will: it catches whatever has been missed.

Review your draft of Maryanne's will section to see how clearly it answers the following questions:

- What's the source of the power Maryanne is trying to exercise?

- Has she followed all the procedural rules Henry established for how to exercise the power?

- Did Henry give Maryanne the power to divide the property the way she has?

- Did Maryanne's disposition require survivorship? Did it leave any gaps?

- Suppose Maryanne ends up being Henry's last surviving descendant. Would it have been useful for Henry to have given her the power to appoint to charity in that situation?

SAMPLE DRAFT

Additional resources, including sample draft documents, are available on the LexisNexis Web Course that was created for this book.

Chapter 14

TRUSTS — FIDUCIARY DUTY

INTRODUCTION

Because a trustee has so much power over assets belonging to others, fiduciary duties and the penalties for violating them give the trustee the incentive not to abuse its discretion and give beneficiaries a remedy for such abuse. There are generally two categories of fiduciary duty: the duty of loyalty and the duty of care. The duty of loyalty requires the trustee to put the best interests of the beneficiaries above the trustee's own personal interests, and the duty of care mandates competent trust administration. The trustor can change the extent of a trustee's duties in the trust document but cannot totally eliminate all fiduciary duty.

An important aspect of the loyalty duty is the requirement that a trustee be impartial in its treatment of different beneficiaries. Unless the trust instrument spells out how to handle conflicts among beneficiaries, the issues can be very difficult to resolve. Conflicts can arise among current income beneficiaries if the trustee has discretion over the amount of distributions to the beneficiaries and one of the beneficiaries is claiming to have more need than others. A more common conflict is between income beneficiaries and remainder beneficiaries who disagree over discretionary distributions to the income beneficiary. For example, if a man had created a trust for the benefit of his wife for life, remainder to the children of the his first marriage, the remaindermen might object to the trustee providing a luxurious retirement home for the spouse, rather than a more austere institution. Investment strategy can also present conflicts. Usually, income beneficiaries prefer that the trustee invest in assets that produce maximum income, and remainder beneficiaries want investments that have the best potential to grow in value over time. For example, if the trust holds improved real property, the income beneficiaries are concerned about maximizing income from the property, but the remaindermen are concerned about spending enough on upkeep so that the property does not fall in value.

If the trustee just depends on his or her judgment to resolve a conflict, the trustee runs the risk of being subject to liability for that judgment many years later. Penalties for violating fiduciary duties can be extreme, and the statute of limitations on when a beneficiary can make a claim of breach can extend over the term of the trust, which may be decades. On the other hand, the trustee can control these risks either by petitioning the court for guidance, allowing the beneficiaries to present their concerns to the court as well, or by attempting to have the beneficiaries reach a compromise agreement.

In this exercise, a trustee who is also the income beneficiary has been challenged by a remainder beneficiary regarding the trustee's choice of investments. The trust term will last for another 10 years, so the trustee wants to resolve the issue with the beneficiary now so that she does not have to worry about a future claim against her. One option would be to request direction from the court, but particularly in the case of choosing investments, mediation is a better option. A court may be reluctant to approve a long-term course of investments, but mediation allows the possibility of the trustee maintaining an amiable relationship with the remainderman and finding a long-term plan that the parties can agree upon.

SKILLS INVOLVED: Mediation skills; issue identification; ethical problem-solving

GENERAL DESCRIPTION OF EXERCISE: Preparing for and conducting a mediation between the income beneficiary of a trust, who is also serving as trustee, and the remainder beneficiary of the same trust. The income and remainder beneficiaries are disagreeing over how to invest the trust property.

PARTICIPANTS NEEDED:

Task 1: One student

Task 2: Three students

ESTIMATED TIME REQUIRED:

Task 1: 1 hour

Task 2: 1 to 2 hours

LEVEL OF DIFFICULTY (1–5):

ROLE IN EXERCISE:

Task 1: You have been selected to act as mediator for a dispute arising out of the Martin Starling Trust and you need to prepare for the mediation by reviewing the memoranda submitted by the parties, reviewing your responsibilities as mediator, and taking notes on talking points that you should raise with each of the parties separately and with the parties jointly.

Task 2: You will go through the mediation, with one student taking the part of mediator and the other two acting as the parties.

THE EXERCISE

TASK 1:

Martin Starling had two children, Beulah and Abigail. Beulah died five years ago in a car accident, leaving one daughter, Heidi. After Beulah's death, Martin altered his Will so that on his death, one-half of his estate would be given outright to Abigail, and the other half was to be placed in trust. Abigail was named trustee and given the right to receive the trust's income during its term The trust is to terminate and the principal distributed to Heidi when she reaches the age of 35 years.

After Martin died two years ago, Abigail, as executor, took her one-half in the form of real estate and part of her father's stock portfolio. She put into the trust the remainder of the stock portfolio and her father's tax-exempt bonds. Currently, 80% of the trust property consists of the tax exempt bonds, and the remainder is invested in stock. Her niece Heidi is now 25 years old. She has challenged her aunt's decision to maintain that large of a percentage of the trust assets in tax exempt bonds because the bonds have little growth potential. Because the trust will last for another ten years, Abigail wants to resolve the issue with Heidi now, and she and Heidi have agreed to mediate their dispute.

You have been appointed as mediator. The parties have each submitted short memoranda that set forth their positions on the issue. Those are set forth below. Review those memoranda, the governing statutes (UTC, Uniform Principal and Income Act and Uniform Prudent Investor Act), and the guidelines for mediators that are posted on the website, and make a list of talking points that you plan to bring up with each of the parties when you speak to them individually, and a list of the talking points and suggestions that you plan to raise with them when you meet with them jointly.

APPLICABLE LAW:

Uniform Trust Code section 803 (stating the duty of impartiality)

Uniform Principal and Income Act

Uniform Prudent Investor Act

MEMORANDA OF PARTIES

Memorandum of Heidi

My grandfather, Martin Starling, had originally intended to give his estate equally to his two children. However, when my mother died, he decided to change his Will to give my mother's one-half to me. My aunt went to visit him and complained to him about her financial situation. She had recently gone through a divorce and it was difficult for her to live on her salary as an elementary school teacher. She also knew that I was going to receive a settlement from the driver who caused my mother's accident. She convinced my grandfather to put my share in trust and let her receive the income from my share until I turned 35. My aunt has left the majority of the money in tax exempt bonds, which works in her favor because she would be the one paying income taxes on the trust income. Also, the bonds pay a steady rate of interest but do not grow in value over time. Due to inflation, the principal will actually be worth less in real dollars when I receive the money at age 35 than what it was worth when the trust was set up.

This type of investment violates several of her fiduciary duties. First, she has the duty to treat the income beneficiary and remainder beneficiary impartially. Second, as trustee she is to put the beneficiaries' interests over her own, and as a beneficiary as well as trustee she has a conflict of interest. Third, under the Uniform Prudent Investor Act, she is supposed to evaluate trust assets shortly after the trust was funded as to whether they are appropriate for the trust purposes. Next, she has a duty to diversify.

My purpose in the mediation is to have my aunt agree to liquidate the bonds and reinvest in assets that not only are relatively safe, but also show a balanced risk and a potential for appreciation.

<u>Memorandum of Abigail</u>

When my father revised his Will after my sister's death, he knew that my share of his estate would not likely be sufficient to insure me a comfortable lifestyle due to my reduced financial situation, and he also knew that my niece would be provided for as a result of the lawsuit brought on her behalf after my sister's death. He did not want to deprive my niece of a share of his estate, however. He compromised by providing me with a right to the income from the funds until my niece turned 35. At the time of my death, he had a significant amount of investments in tax exempt bonds and encouraged me to keep those investments because he was mistrustful of the safety of the stock market and he wanted to be sure the principal for my niece would be safe. He told me this, and told me that he was making me trustee so that I could control the investments to be sure that I was receiving adequate income.

Article 12 of my father's will, listing the trustee's powers and duties, states that the trustee has the authority to retain original investments and to invest and reinvest assets in any way the trustee deems advisable." Therefore, the document setting up the trust evidences my father's intentions, as he explained them to me, that I had the power to favor my interest as the income beneficiary and to retain the bonds as a valid trust investment. The Uniform Prudent Investor Act provides that the trustor can override duties under the Act.

My purpose in the mediation is to arrive at an investment plan that my niece will accept while still following my father's intentions.

TASK 2:

Review the materials for Task 1,including the relevant statutes and the materials on mediation on the website. Assign the roles of mediator, Abigail and Heidi, and meet for the mediation. The mediator first meets with the parties, explains the mediator's role, and allows each party to give a brief statement of her position. Then the parties are separated into separate rooms, and the mediator meets separately with the parties, making suggestions and bringing offers and counter offers to the parties until an agreement is reached or until it is clear that no agreement is possible. If agreement is reached, the mediator and the parties should then draw up a short agreement setting forth the basic terms of the agreement.

RESOURCES

Additional resources are available on the LexisNexis Web Course that was created for this book.

Andersen, *Understanding Trusts and Estates* § 55[A] (4th ed.)

Uniform Trust Code § 803

Uniform Principal and Income Act

Uniform Prudent Investor Act

**DO NOT PROCEED TO THE NEXT PAGE UNTIL YOU HAVE
COMPLETED THE EXERCISE**

SELF-STUDY

TASK 1:

- What was your conclusion regarding the legal issue of whether the trustee had a duty to change the trust assets? Were you convinced by the quoted language and the father's statements that she could retain the bonds without consideration of whether they were appropriate? Even if the trust did not authorize her to retain the bonds, would the language of the statutes require her to sell them or can she justify keeping them under those standards? Note that in many states' statutes give trustees the authority to retain inception assets, so she would have had a better argument in those states. Examples of such statutes are linked on the website.

- How did you plan to deal with Heidi's apparent resentment of her aunt's role in Martin's estate plan? One of the goals of mediation should be to improve the relationship of the parties, particularly in such a situation where the parties will continue to deal with each other for a long period of time.

- Were you able to think of alternative investment methods? This may be easier for students who have financial experience. Your advice might vary depending on the state of the financial markets at the time that you are doing this exercise. One suggestion, however, may have occurred to you based on the terms of the Uniform Principal and Income Act. That statute allows a trustee to convert a trust (with court approval) into a total return trust. A total return trust would give Abigail a set return based on the value of the trust assets, rather than being tied to the actual income of the trust. Such an arrangement would reduce the tension because both Abigail and Heidi would both benefit with a higher value of the underlying principal.

TASK 2:

- The success of this exercise will depend on how vigorously the parties take on their roles and assert their interests. It is difficult to get the experience of an actual mediation when there are no real life interests at stake, and the time is relatively limited. However, the exercise is intended to give an opportunity for you to get a sense of the creativity and diplomacy necessary to mediate.

- Not all mediations result in agreements, but Abigail should have a strong motivation to reach agreement because she is vulnerable to breach of duty claims asserted by Heidi. If Heidi remains unhappy, she is likely to watch Abigail closely and raise other potential claims against Abigail in addition to this issue of the tax exempt bonds. In addition, Heidi's young age, the tragedy of her mother's death and her resentment of her aunt may make her less amenable to settlement. Any agreement would therefore be likely to lean in Heidi's favor.

- All students participating should keep in mind that there are considerations other than money. The family relationship between Heidi and Abigail, particularly in view of their lost family members, should be a very important factor.

Chapter 15

PLANNING FOR DISABILITY

INTRODUCTION

Estate planners regularly recommend that their clients execute durable powers of attorney (DPA's) authorizing others (an agent-in-fact) to act in the clients' (the principal) behalf during periods of the clients' incapacity. The paths to such a recommendation, however, vary in both their direction and the issues raised along the way.

Some clients come in for a will and are skeptical when a lawyer also suggests creating a power of attorney. They wonder: "Is this lawyer just trying to sell me another product, like the maintenance agreement to a computer?" In good health at the time, they many not have thought much about the consequences of temporary (let alone long-term) disability. Questions like "Who could cash your paycheck if you were in a serious accident?" can get the conversation going.

Other clients come in the door asking for a "standard" power of attorney. Although appreciating the utility of executing a DPA, these clients may need prompting to consider questions like who would be the best choice to hold such a power. For example, their seemingly good-hearted neighbor may become sorely tempted when given access to someone else's money. Clients should be especially aware of the danger in creating conflicts of interest. Naming a son or daughter may seem like the best idea until the client considers that the child may be reluctant to spend money on the parent's behalf, so more will be left in an eventual estate. Another issue is expertise. However well-intentioned, an agent-in-fact may be overmatched by insurance claim forms or the need to make investment decisions.

One of the most difficult circumstances occurs when a younger person brings in an elderly person to get a DPA naming the younger person. Two issues predominate. First, you must establish that you are representing the (older) person who would be executing the power. Second, you must be confident that the client has the sufficient mental capacity to execute the power and is not acting under undue influence (especially from the person who would become the agent-in-fact). *See* CPR §§ 1.2(f) (prohibiting a lawyer from willfully purporting to act as a lawyer for any person without the authority of that person) and 1.13 (requiring a lawyer to determine whether a client's ability to make adequately considered decisions in connection with the representation is impaired). Techniques like those discussed in Chapter 6 can be useful in this context as well.

In terms of the DPA itself, the biggest problem is that third parties — banks, insurance companies, stock brokers — may not honor the power. Concerned that a person claiming to be an agent may not really have the authority to act, those third parties may simply refuse to cooperate. Fortunately, good planning can protect against the principal objections third parties are likely to raise. If they ask whether the principal had the mental capacity to create the power, a lawyer might have available in the file a notarized statement from witnesses attesting to the client's capacity and the absence of undue influence. A DPA specifically granting comprehensive powers usually can allay fears that a particular activity is not authorized. Some of the less-common activities that a client may want to authorize are: filing and paying taxes, signing a lease or buying a house, changing domicile, selling a business, and making gifts. Gifts can be a special problem, because some agents-in-fact have been very generous in transferring their principals' property into their own names. DPA's should limit clearly the scope of any gift-making authority. Also, many DPA's authorize agents to obtain medical information protected by the Health Insurance Portability and Accountability Act [HIPAA], 42 U.S.C. § 1320(d).

So-called "springing" powers create special problems. These are DPA's that are not effective until an event — usually the disability of the principal — takes place. In other words, there is no power until it is needed. In any situation, the question then becomes whether the condition kicking in the power has taken place. Perhaps the best way to avoid the problem is not to use a springing power at all. Some clients say they like the idea of a springing power because they don't trust their agents-in-fact not to use a presently-exercisable power while the clients can still handle their own affairs. The best response is: if you don't trust the person who would be your agent, choose another agent.

A springing DPA might be appropriate, however, in some situations, like when family harmony might better be preserved if no one had any power until the last possible moment. If a client wants to create a springing power, the document should define "disabled" and probably should identify a group of people (with flexible membership) to decide whether the principal meets the definition. Including a HIPAA authorization is especially important in that context. To relieve any third party's concerns about whether the power had indeed sprung into action, you might attach a statement from the group certifying the incapacity.

Because DPA's are always revocable while the principal is competent, third parties can never be sure that the power presented hasn't been revoked moments before. There's no perfect solution, but encouraging your clients to execute new documents periodically should give third parties more confidence. If the client has become incapacitated, you can attach a statement from credible witnesses that the principal is no longer competent and, to their knowledge, the power has never been revoked. Also, some third parties will take comfort from a statement that they will not be held liable if they honor the document in good faith, believing that it had not been revoked.

SKILLS INVOLVED: Planning factual investigation, following ethical standards, developing strategies, drafting.

GENERAL DESCRIPTION OF EXERCISE: Preparation for a client meeting and drafting of a durable power of attorney

PARTICIPANTS NEEDED: This is an individual exercise to be completed by one student.

ESTIMATED TIME REQUIRED:

Task 1: 20–30 minutes

Task 2: 60–90 minutes

LEVEL OF DIFFICULTY (1–5):

ROLE IN EXERCISE: Prepare for a meeting with an elderly man and his niece, and then draft his durable power of attorney.

THE EXERCISE

TASK 1:   Your administrative assistant has set aside an hour next week for you to meet with Bhadra Kapoor and her uncle, Lakshanya Patel. Kapoor called to set up the appointment because Patel needs a Power of Attorney. You've never met either of them. Draft a memo for the file creating a checklist on how you want to conduct the meeting, including topics you plan to raise.

TASK 2:   At your meeting, you learned that Patel has created an unfunded Life Insurance Trust naming Second Bank as Trustee. Currently the trust has no assets. Patel expects it to remain empty until his death, when proceeds from his life insurance will fund the trust. However, the trust does provide that if funds are added during his lifetime, then the trustee will manage those funds to benefit him. The trust is identified as "The Lakshanya Patel Trust" and was executed on September 16, 20XX [four years ago]

Patel has decided to execute a Durable Power of Attorney, naming Bhadra Kapoor as agent and Patel's nephew, Danvir Gupta, as successor. In addition to standard authority, Patel wants to authorize the agent to add funds to the trust at Second Bank. That could be useful if he ends up with a long-term disability. Also, Patel wants the agent to be able to make gifts to family members. No gift can exceed the then-effective annual exclusion amount for gift taxes, nor can the total of all gifts in any year exceed 10% of the value of his total assets. Draft a presently-effective Durable Power of Attorney for Patel.

REFERENCES

Additional resources are available on the LexisNexis Web Course that was created for this book.

Rules of Professional Conduct §§ 1.2(f), 1.6 and 1.13

Roger W. Andersen, *Understanding Trusts & Estates* §§ 22[B], 61[B] (4th ed. 2009)

Roger W. Andersen, *Plan While You Can: Legal Solutions for Facing Disability (2003)* Ch. 3

Karen E. Boxx, *The Durable Power of Attorney's Place in the Family of Fiduciary Relationships,* 36 GEORGIA L. REV. 1 (2001)

DO NOT PROCEED TO THE NEXT PAGE UNTIL YOU HAVE COMPLETED THE EXERCISE

SELF-STUDY

<u>TASK 1:</u> Check to see if your checklist includes:

- Clarify that Patel would be your client. Meet with Patel alone. Establish competence & lack of undue influence. If marginal, build a record. Discuss whether he wants to waive confidentiality. Obtain a waiver.

- Discuss whether a presently-effective or springing power. If springing on incompetence, discuss drawbacks, identify procedure for deciding incompetent. HIPAA authorization?

- Discuss — privately — whether Kapoor is qualified. Identify a successor and discuss qualifications.

- Include powers to make gifts? To Kapoor? To charity? Any limits on donees or size?

- Any unusual powers needed? Spending for pets? Amending a trust or a community property agreement?

<u>TASK 2:</u>

- Can you eliminate words? Can you find "in the event that" or "on the condition that"? Both mean "if." When you read a list of various powers, can you select one word that covers all or some of the others (and eliminate them)?

- Did you include helpful headings? Would different categorizations increase clarity? Would tabulation of various powers increase clarity?

- Are the references to Patel's trust clear?

- Does the authorization to make gifts to Kapoor overcome any conflict of interest objections? Are limits clearly stated? Will they change as the gift tax annual exclusion changes?

Chapter 16

ESTATE AND GIFT TAXATION

INTRODUCTION

This exercise is intended to give you only a general introduction to federal estate and gift taxation. Many trust and estates classes cover the subject, albeit briefly, because so many estate planning decisions are based on tax considerations, and therefore the estate plans that show up in the cases in the textbook often contain elements that were the result of tax planning.

This exercise will require you to fill out an estate tax return for a relatively straightforward estate. Calculating the estate tax for a particular set of facts will give you a more specific understanding of the underlying mechanics of the tax and how the gift and estate tax work together. The federal estate tax and gift tax are coordinated, even though they are not "unified" as they had been previously. The federal estate tax is meant to apply only to larger estates. Therefore, there is an exemption amount (called the "exemption equivalent") that passes tax free, and the tax is imposed only on the assets in the estate over that amount. If a person dies in 2009, when the exemption equivalent is $3.5 million, and that person leaves a $4 million estate (net of deductions), then only the $500,000 over the exemption equivalent is subject to the tax. The exemption equivalent can be used to some extent during life. For example, you can choose to make lifetime gifts up to the maximum allowed for lifetime gifts (as of this writing, $1 million), and use any remainder of the total exemption equivalent at death.

One other factor to keep in mind when coordinating the gift and estate tax is the annual exclusion. Gifts up to the annual exclusion amount (which is a number indexed to inflation and was $12,000 in 2008), are not considered taxable. There are many conditions on this nontaxable treatment, but there is no limit on the number of qualifying annual exclusion gifts a taxpayer can make in a year. For example, if Taxpayer A gave $10,000 cash to each of her 13 grandchildren, none of those gifts would be taxable. If Taxpayer A gave $22,000 to each of those 13 grandchildren at a time when the annual exclusion amount was $12,000, then she would have made total taxable gifts of $130,000. At her death, her exemption equivalent would be reduced by $130,000 because of the lifetime *taxable* gifts, but the $156,000 in annual exclusion gifts would not be subtracted from the exemption equivalent.

ONE CAVEAT: Federal estate and gift taxation is, like most taxes, politically controversial and therefore subject to change. Another aspect of the exercise that is subject to change is the value of the stock listed as part of the estate, which you will have to determine in order to complete the exercise. This exercise is drafted to accommodate some market fluctuations as well as changes in the tax rates and exemption amounts but not any significant structural changes to the tax law. Because of the online component of these materials, we are able to provide a completed estate tax form on the website as part of the self-study materials that will be updated each year to the current form and that will reflect current tax rates and exemption levels. **Before beginning the exercise, however, you should check the website for this chapter for any edits to the facts that are necessary to accommodate current conditions.**

As a final comment, in practice most estate tax returns are prepared using software that asks a series of questions. Instead, for this exercise you will be working only with the form and instructions and completing it "by hand." The advantage of this approach is that you will be able to see how the form works, and when reviewing a return completed by software, you will be better equipped to find errors.

SKILLS INVOLVED: Fact analysis and development, working with forms, tax research

GENERAL DESCRIPTION OF EXERCISE: Preparation of federal estate tax return

PARTICIPANTS NEEDED: This is an individual exercise to be completed by one student.

ESTIMATED TIME REQUIRED:

90 minutes

LEVEL OF DIFFICULTY (1–5):

ROLE IN EXERCISE: You are acting as lawyer for the estate of Dora Mora, and will be completing the federal estate tax return for her estate.

APPLICABLE LAW: Assume that there is no state estate or inheritance tax in Dora Mora's state of residence. The current law regarding federal estate and gift tax as of the year you are completing the exercise will be the applicable law. Because of the simplified facts, you should be able to complete the return using the Form 706 and Instructions found on the website for the Internal Revenue Service.

THE EXERCISE

Dora Mora died on January 6 of this year. She was a U.S. citizen, and has lived in Springfield, State for her entire life. At the time of Dora's death, she was living at 244 Boat Street, Springfield, State. The house was purchased during Dora's marriage to Herbert, who died on September 1, 1990, and she inherited it from his estate. Herbert's Social Security number was 000-44-2222. Dora was born on November 7, 1942, and her Social Security No. is 000-34-0120. Dora's probate proceedings are pending in Columbia County Superior Court under cause number 10-4-3367. Dora died testate. Surviving her are her two daughters, Sophie Mora and Giovanna Mora. Sophie is serving as Personal Representative of her estate. Sophie lives at 1400 Lakeview Drive and her phone number is (000) 123-4567. Sophie's SSN is 000-34-1111, and Giovanna's SSN is 000-34-2222.

Dora's Will leaves $200,000 to the Columbia County Audubon Society, with the remainder of her estate to be distributed in equal shares to her daughters.

In 1990, after Herbert's death, Dora gave each of the daughters $100,000. Appropriate gift tax returns were filed. (HINT: back then, the annual exclusion amount was $10,000).

Dora's assets consist of the following:

1. The home legally described as Lot 1, University Addition, situate in Columbia County, State, which was valued as of date of death at $835,000.

2. 212,500 shares of Microsoft common stock, 200 shares of Berkshire Hathaway Class A common and 5,000 shares of common stock of Walmart.

3. a 5 year old Volvo worth $4,000.

4. Household furnishings worth approximately $15,000.

5. A bank account, at Bedford Savings Bank, in the name of Dora and Sophie as joint tenants, account number 0276 with a balance of $19,442 and account number 007 with a balance of $4,222.

Dora's funeral cost $5,000. You have determined that your fees as attorney for handling the estate will be $7,000 plus $380 in costs. There were appraiser's fees of $2,000. The accountant's fees will be $6,300.

The following bills were outstanding as of Dora's death:

- Dr. Clooney	$1100
- Nordstrom	315
- Cable Company	67
- Lawn-Dromat Gardening Service	96
- Federal income tax owing	9,345

Miscellaneous:

-   Feel free to make up any missing yet necessary facts.

-   For the Microsoft, Walmart and Berkshire Hathaway stock, look for the approximate values of these stocks on the date of death. The symbols for each of the companies are as follows: Berkshire Hathaway is BRK.A, Microsoft is MSFT and Walmart is WMT. You can find these on the internet; there any number of services that give you stock quotes on the internet. Some links are provided on the website, or you can use your own favorite. Use the closing price on the date of death for each of the stocks. If the date of death falls on a weekend or holiday, or the market was closed on the date of death for any other reason, use the closing price on the last day the market was open before the date of death. **This is not the valuation method required under the instructions to Form 706.** We are using a simplified method for this exercise because obtaining the information in the form required by the IRS can be complicated, and practitioners usually use a valuation service for the information put onto the return. The purpose of having you look up the values with the simplified method is to introduce you to valuation resources and give you the skills necessary for the preliminary work on a tax return, which would include an estimated value of assets.

RESOURCES

Andersen, *Understanding Trusts and Estates* Chapter 14 (4th ed.)

The LexisNexis Web Course that was created for this book includes links to the IRS website, to IRS Form 706, and to the instructions for Form 706. Read all instructions carefully.

DO NOT PROCEED TO THE NEXT PAGE UNTIL YOU HAVE COMPLETED THE EXERCISE

SELF-STUDY

- A sample completed estate tax return, with annotations, is on the website.

- Did you realize that the form must be filled out "backwards"? In other words, you have to fill out the schedules first in order to be able to fill out the tax calculations on the first and second pages. Many tax returns operate this way. Did you list the joint bank account on Schedule E, jointly owned property? The facts did not specify whether any part of the funds in the account were contributed by Sophie. However, the instructions require that the entire value of the account be included except to the extent you could prove that Sophie contributed the funds. In other words, with respect to joint tenancy property, the burden is on the estate to prove that not all the property was contributed by the decedent.

- Did you deduct $10,000 from each gift to the daughters? The amount that should have been included on line 4 of the first page is $180,000 ($100,000 less $10,000 for each of the two daughters).

- Did you understand how the lifetime gifts plus the estate were considered together for the tax calculation? The form requires you to add the value of lifetime gifts to the value of the estate. It then subtracts the full value of the exemption equivalent, and then calculates the tax due on the remaining amount.

- Did you deduct the gift to the Audubon Society on Schedule O? All qualifying charitable gifts are deducted from the estate to be taxed. If a testator died with a $12 million estate, and gave it all to charity, there would be no estate tax.